What Other People Are Saying

Incredibly, you spend years in school preparing for a career that can be compromised in a few moments with improper behavior. Manners do matter — no matter how informal the business environment. The good news is that Colleen's book is an etiquette boot camp for avoiding social and business pitfalls. *Be On Your Best Business Behavior* is an informative and entertaining tool for any of us who have wondered (and worried) about the proper way to do anything — and in any situation.

— Jeff Singsaas
General Manager
Microsoft Corporation

Being schooled in proper business etiquette is essential in today's fast-paced and diverse business community. Colleen attacks the subject with a "hands-on" manner, walks a group through all the steps needed in making a business dinner or meeting a success. She also makes it more than a learning experience, she makes it a fun and enjoyable time with her. The results are immediate as you can see positive changes and real confidence grow with your executives as they conduct themselves much differently at business dinners and meetings following the Colleen Rickenbacher experience.

— Jim DeLong
Vice President, Sales and National Accounts
Bayer CropScience LP

Psst! Your manners are showing! Even with today's more casual workplace, it's imperative that we still "mind our manners." And Colleen Rickenbacher, who personifies every facet of being the best in business, is a great teacher. Her timely book is clear and precise, her message refreshing. So enjoy the pleasant journey to being on your best business behavior!

— Edward E. Scannell, CMP, CSP
Co-author "Games Trainers Play" McGraw-Hill series
Director, Center for Professional Development and Training

Whether presented in person or in her new book, Colleen Rickenbacher's message is universal. Her ideas are adaptable from an everyday business dinner to a meeting with a four-star general. Colleen's material has been not only informative and educational for our cheerleaders but also fun! We love her enthusiasm and zeal for her topics and her interactive presentations. This book is a winner!

— Kelli McGonagill Finglass
Director, Dallas Cowboys Cheerleaders

I had the pleasure of having Colleen Rickenbacher as the keynote speaker at our "Celebrating Women in the Workplace" event, where she shared many of the things addressed in her book. We found these suggestions to be a must-have for all women — single, married, widowed, housewife, mother, career woman. Colleen's energetic and enthusiastic way of communicating the information makes it fun and exciting to learn how to be at our best with confidence.

— Lindsay Roberts
First Lady of Oral Roberts University

BE ON YOUR BEST
BUSINESS
BEHAVIOR

BE ON YOUR BEST
BUSINESS
BEHAVIOR

HOW TO AVOID SOCIAL
AND PROFESSIONAL FAUX PAS
WHEN DINING, TRAVELING, CONVERSING
AND ENTERTAINING

Colleen A. Rickenbacher, CMP, CSEP, CPC

BE ON YOUR BEST BUSINESS BEHAVIOR
© 2007 Colleen Rickenbacher

Cover photograph: Nick Dolding/ Getty Images

Manufactured in the United States of America

For Information, please contact:
www.colleenrickenbacher.com

ISBN 0-9713265-6-8
LCCN 2004101934
2 3 4 5 6 7 8 9 10

Dedication

To my family…
You are the absolute best and
thanks for always supporting me
in everything I do.

Contents

● ● ● ● ● ● ● ●

Acknowledgments

Thanks to Laurie Sprouse, CITE, DMCP, CMP, Ultimate Ventures, Inc. Dallas, Texas, for her packing list adapted for Chapter Eleven.

Also appreciation goes to the Dallas Police Department and National Fire Protection Association for background for Chapter Fourteen.

Finally, my husband Steve, and daughter Andrea, for their excellent support, Linda Chandler for her editing skills and Tim Cocklin, CSL, CCF, Worlds of Wonder, for getting the book ready for publishing.

Introduction

Etiquette is like clothes for women. You need to update and keep with the latest trends. Etiquette is very stylish but you may need to be reminded at times of things your mother or someone special in your life might have taught you many years ago. Possibly you just forgot these little lessons of kindness or just pushed them aside for awhile. So it is time to bring them back. Etiquette is being polite, respectful and considerate of others. So it is pretty basic and easy to make etiquette a part of your day-to-day activities. It could be something as simple as a thank-you to the wait staff in a restaurant, allowing people to exit the elevator before you jump in, holding the door for a total stranger or to allowing a driver to enter from a side road. Hopefully they will signal a thanks back to you. Etiquette starts with your own family and then extends to friends and work associates. So spread the goodness and kind gestures. Remember that people learn from their environment. So try and pass on a little etiquette to everyone you touch.

Etiquette even involves people that you may see or meet only once. It doesn't take any more time to smile at a person as they pass you on the street or even exchange a few words with a total stranger that you sit next to in a waiting room or lobby. The best etiquette is to turn off your cell phone as you enter an establishment, pull through a drive-through window or check out at a grocery store. Give people your full attention and that can be your best gift of kindness. No matter who they may be, they all deserve a warm thank you, a kind smile and possibly even a handwritten thank-you note for certain occasions.

Etiquette is respect for others and kindness that you show. Everything I am sharing with you in this book is either a rule developed and adopted over time or my suggestion. But please remember that these are guidelines and tips for you to use as needed. If your mother, aunt or close friend has taught you another way, never mess with mothers and their rearing skills.

Speaking, teaching and training people about proper etiquette and protocol started out just trying to make my former office and company a little better in dining situations. Well, that first training session to my own co-workers back in 1996 opened the door for me to pursue this career in speaking and writing. From my first etiquette program to now it has been so enjoyable and rewarding. I get to watch people in my training classes or presentations say "aah" or "I didn't know that" or even worse "I have done this wrong my entire life." I decided that I wanted my sessions and seminars to make people feel good about themselves and then to share it with everyone around them. It may be the way you look, exchanging your business cards or just feeling comfortable in any dining situation. It is nice when you look at your table setting and know that you will not be picking up someone's coffee cup, using their napkin or placing your buttered roll on their bread and butter plate. People deal with people that they enjoy, they want to work with, and also appreciate. It doesn't really matter if you sit up perfectly straight or you do everything properly. What does matter is how you conduct yourself in all situations both personally and professionally. Etiquette breeds better working conditions, a happier family and a better you. Again, remember that etiquette sets you apart and increases your overall effectiveness.

I want to extend my deepest appreciation to my husband, Steve, for allowing me to spend endless hours at my computer and also our three children, Andrea, Lauren and Jon, for always being there. I also want to thank everyone that bought the first and second editions of this book or booked me to do a speech or training program or for giving me the necessary kudos to keep writing and to improve myself. So to all of you, I extend my deepest thanks and appreciation. Please enjoy this book.

ONE

Looking Your Best For Business

● ● ● ● ● ● ●

Did you know you have only three to five seconds to make a good first impression? It may not seem fair, but your appearance speaks for you before you can express your thoughts. What you wear influences others and can make you feel more confident and in control. Focus on being appropriately dressed every day. That client you've been courting for months may suddenly have an open lunch date and you'll need to be ready on a moment's notice.

Clothes and their formality, or lack of, have changed drastically over the past 10 to 15 years and the whole dotcom revolution. In the past the only accepted dress for the office was a coat, shirt and tie or dress and even stockings/pantyhose for the women. Now you can find khaki pants, capri pants, exposed skin, cleavage, belly views and even rubber flip flops.

Many surveys have been conducted and employers and employees are still arguing the value of attire and the end result on the work level. Legal issues and discrimination with many of these decisions are being settled in court. I strongly agree we all need to be creative, but looking like you spent a little time in preparing for work or a social function is certain to make a good impression. Remember what may be "creative," may just be downright lazy and pushing the envelope.

Successful Dressing and Image

- Wear appropriate clothes for each occasion. Respect dress codes. If you are unsure about what to wear, call and ask the host or someone who knows the dress code or the proper attire. If the host tells you to wear "whatever you want" then ask what they plan to wear. It will provide a gauge of the formality of the event. When in doubt, dress conservatively. For work, take cues from senior employees or your supervisor. It is always better to be a little over-dressed than under-dressed.
- Dress how you want to be perceived. In the workplace, those who dress professionally may be more likely to catch the attention of upper management and to be seen as candidates for better positions.
- Be recognized but for the right reasons.
- Dress for your shape, your personality, your needs and your age. Develop a consistent style that takes into account your size and shape. Avoid attire that makes you feel uncomfortable. You don't have to have expensive clothes to create a good look.
- Update your clothes regularly. If you still look like you did 10 years ago, it's time for a make-over. Get rid of clothes you haven't worn within at least the last 18 months or for the past two seasons. Chances are you will not wear those clothes again. Give them away or try selling them at a resale or consignment store. Then with the money you receive, buy new items.
- Don't worry about trends. They come and go quickly and you won't get your money's worth for that garment you just had to have. Besides, not everyone looks good in

trendy fashions. Make sure your body is "hip and trendy" before you put on those "hip and trendy" clothes.

- Go for quality over quantity. A few great, well-made items will last a lot longer than random, less expensive clothes.
- Shoes are critical. Again, a few well-made shoes will work with your professional and personal wardrobe. Always keep them clean, shined and well heeled.
- Don't wait until the last minute to plan your wardrobe choices. You will start the day feeling better if you haven't hurried deciding what to wear in the morning. Put your clothes out the night before with all accessories. And this includes ironing your clothes and polishing your shoes. You are allowed to change your mind in the morning, but at least you have a starting point.
- Take your time shopping. If you need something for a special occasion, shop for it in advance. Don't shop under pressure. If you shop at the last moment, you may not be pleased with your selection and your appearance may not send the right message. You may also end up spending more money because you need the outfit and have to buy what is available.
- Make sure your clothes are never stained, wrinkled or missing buttons. Runs in panty hose or slight holes are unacceptable. These things detract from your best overall look.
- Never forget the importance of good grooming to your overall appearance. Your hair, nails, makeup and personal hygiene should always be top on your list.
- Attention to detail is the key. Accessories can dress up an outfit and help you express your personality. Just be careful not to overdo it. Simple can be beautiful.
- Always check your appearance from all angles in a full-length mirror before leaving home (and when exiting a restroom).

- Make sure all tags are tucked in. Nothing ruins "the look" more than a tag hanging out.

Necessities to Help with Your Image

- A nice jacket or sweater
- A pair of good shoes
- One piece of nice jewelry
- A quality watch
- A nice wallet, handbag or briefcase
- Lint brush (Keep one at home, in your car, in your desk and in your travel bag.)
- Sewing kit (One in your travel bag also)
- Iron and ironing board
- Full-length mirror
- Shoe polish (Also have a polish sponge for travel. A lot of hotels will make these available as one of their amenities. Use them.)

Makeup

- You are going to work, not appearing on stage. Don't overdo it with your makeup for the office. Keep it light during the day. A nice moisturizer and foundation are a good start. A little powder, blush, eyeliner, mascara and lipstick should do the trick.
- Select the blends and colors that bring out your highlights and compliment your skin color.
- We all have "natural beauty," but a little makeup is still a good idea.
- Remember to allow enough time each morning to apply

makeup. Don't apply it in your car as you are arriving in the parking lot or, even worse, don't put on your makeup at your desk.

Hair

- Your hairstyle should be appropriate for your facial shape, hair type, personality, profession and lifestyle. It should be complimentary to you and easy for you to take care of.
- Do not come to work with your hair partially dry or style your hair at your desk.
- Consider your hairstyle periodically. Is the style too young-looking for your age or does it make you look too old? When is the last time you changed your hair style? It might be time.
- The condition of your hair is also important for your overall professional look. Keep it trimmed and styled.
- Women, watch what you wear in your hair, including scrunchies and clips. Those may be great for the weekend or a nice hike in the mountains but not for your office appearance. Choose hair accessories that lend a more polished look. Always ask the question, "Would that clip be better on a potato chip bag or in my hair?"
- For men gray hair becomes distinguished. Gray hair for women shouts aging, but you have options. A good, stylish cut can flatter silver or graying hair. It is best to consult a stylist before you decide to test hair colors on your own hair.
- Dandruff is common. If you have it, use special shampoos and treatments and make it go away.

Handbags

- Your handbag or purse should suit you. Make sure that your handbag is not too large and inappropriate for your size. Small clutch bags are more appropriate for evening and special occasions.
- You do not need to carry everything you own with you in your purse. You can leave some personal items in your desk drawer or at home.
- The handbag should be durable and coordinated with your clothes and your style.
- One good work handbag is appropriate so you don't have to change out the items every day.
- Don't look like the "bag person" with two or three bags over your shoulder. Condense to one bag for meetings.

Feet and Shoes

- Is an open-toed sandal that you would wear to the beach appropriate for work? I don't think so. Even with some offices in the business casual mode, that is still too casual. Watch what you put on your feet.
- Men should wear socks to work. Even if you have a nice shirt and slacks, wearing no socks takes your outfit about 10 steps lower. A nice lightweight sock would be more appropriate.
- All shoes should be good quality, shined and in good condition. Shoes should not be scuffed and the heels should not be worn down.
- If women are able to wear a nice, dressy sandal, then no panty hose. Remember open-toed shoes means open-toed. Do not wear panty hose or socks with sandals.

- A nice leather sandal with a low heel can change a casual look to a business casual.
- But should you go bare-legged? If so, then do it tastefully. Have your skirt at a decent length and make sure your sandals are dressy and appropriate for the workplace. If your legs are extremely pale, have veins or are on the heavier side, opt for hosiery and forget the sandals.
- If you do go for the open-toed sandal look, then make sure your toes are ready for display. They must be manicured and polished. No matter how pretty the sandal, some toes should not be exposed to the public.
- Men please remember that the appearance of your feet is also very important. The professional pedicure may not be for you (but you should try it). You still need to make sure that your feet and especially toes look good in your sandals.
- If you do wear sandals, 99 percent of the time you should not have socks on. I am still searching for that one percent when you should!

Bare Arms

- Bare arms are considered very casual, and in most offices arms should be covered.
- If you wear a sleeveless blouse or sweater/shell, tie a cardigan sweater over your shoulders as a cover up. A light weight jacket could also be worn to complete a more professional look.
- Watch the size of your arms and consider if a nice sleeve would be more appropriate and complimentary to your figure. A three-quarter length sleeve would draw more attention to your wrist and away from the upper part of your arm.

A Few Hints

- Beware of fads and fashion trends. If they don't fit your lifestyle or your body style, save your money for more suitable outfits that will endure more than one season.
- Do not wear clothes that are too tight, too short or too low. They will have a tendency to make you look heavier and shorter.
- Fingernails should be manicured and polished. Long, dark-colored nails with designs are not appropriate for the office.
- Remove hats when you enter a building, office or home. Just turning that baseball cap around does not count.
- Men, make sure that your belt matches your shoes.
- Men should not wear short socks that reveal leg when they sit down. The socks do not have to be up to your knee but should be long enough to cover your leg when you sit down. If not, check the length of your pants!
- You also want the socks to compliment your outfit. Create a nice long look with the sock just continuing the outfit and overall look. It was always said that the closest item to your shoes should match your shoes. Not necessarily so. You want a continuous look from your shirt to the pants and then the socks and shoes. Don't break up the look with a lighter color pants and then dark socks. Coordinate for the best overall look.
- Ties for men have become bolder and more expressive, which is great and creative, but be sure your office or meetings are ready for this creativity. If not, a classic stylish tie will always work. Make sure your tie is long enough. It should reach the belt, with the narrow end even

8

with or a little bit shorter than the wide end. Tall or large men should buy extra long ties. Remember to touch the middle of your belt for the perfect length.

- Remember, men, when you sit down to eat, the tie remains in the center of your body. Do not flip it over your shoulder or tuck it into your shirt. Not a good first impression.
- A man should be well groomed, with any facial hair neatly trimmed.
- You want your first impression to be your best.

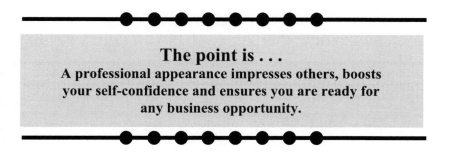

The point is . . .
A professional appearance impresses others, boosts your self-confidence and ensures you are ready for any business opportunity.

TWO

Mastering Communication Technology

━━━━━ ●━●━●━●━●━●━● ━━━━━

Computerized office environments, telecommuting and all the electronic innovations of the past two decades have created a new set of situations to challenge professional behavior. As handy as some electronic tools can be, they also create irritation and interruptions. A business professional should know how to balance well-mannered attention to a client against a ringing cell phone. Shame on you if you don't! The most important thing to remember is who is more important. The person you are talking to on the phone or the person sitting next to you?

E-mail

- E-mail is still a business communication. Watch grammar, spelling and abbreviations. People will judge your e-mail just as critically as all other business transactions.
- Use the subject line. Your subject line needs to grab the reader instantly so they will open and respond. Keep the subject short and to the point. It could be the most important part of your e-mail.
- All lowercasing or all caps is difficult to read. Using all capital letters is considered the equivalent of shouting. All lowercase is not whispering, but it is annoying.
- Don't use e-mail when a handwritten note is more appropriate. (See Chapter Five on thank-you notes.)
- If you get a request addressed to numerous people, respond only to the sender unless requested to do otherwise.

- Read all your e-mails before responding. Go to the most recent ones first and you may discover earlier messages have been amended or updated.
- Be careful of your password. Protect it.
- Be discreet about sending jokes and other questionable comments. You never know who may receive or pass on something you thought would remain private. The best advice I have ever heard was "if it can be written on a postcard then it is safe to send."
- Respond to e-mails or ask to be removed from unwanted routing lists. Twenty-four hours or less is a good standard policy for responding to your e-mails.
- Some companies can and will monitor employee e-mail. Legally, employers have the right to read all employee e-mail on their computer systems. Make sure you understand your office policy on e-mail and personal correspondence.
- Consider the length of your e-mail. A good policy is if your text is two-thirds of the screen, you might want to consider an attachment. Keep e-mail short because so many people are now reading them from hand-held devices and attachments are a little more difficult and generally a slower process.
- Watch all emotional signs. Happy faces and other characters do not belong on a business communication.
- Exclamation points and ellipses should not be used excessively in your business e-mail. But in a less formal e-mail if you need to convey a little more excitement or a partial omission, then they can be used. But don't go over board… if you know what I mean!

- You can sometimes stop e-mail after it has been sent (if done before the recipient reads it), but even if you delete your e-mail, it does not go away forever. It can be recovered and traced.
- Don't let e-mail (or any other written form of communication) substitute for discussing important issues in person. I don't think you want to fire an employee via e-mail.
- Can an e-mail be used instead of a handwritten thank-you note? At times. It is always better to go for the handwritten note but for a quick response an e-mail thank-you is appropriate. It could be ok to send a quick note to thank someone initially for a gift but it is still absolutely important to follow up with that handwritten note.
- If e-mailing internationally, keep the language as formal as possible. Casual language, clichés, jargon and slang words or phrases may have different meanings elsewhere.
- Make sure you have a "signature line" at the end of your e-mail message. I don't mean your name written in cursive but a quick reference including your full name, title, company, phone, fax, e-mail and Web site. Make it easy for people to contact you instantly.
- If you are out of your office for an extended time, use the "Out of Office" message so people are aware that you might not be available to respond instantly. You can also provide information on your message about your return, another way to contact you if necessary and any other details, but keep your message short and concise. If "Out of the Office" is not on your computer system or not permitted by your company then alternate plans to handle your incoming e-mail should be addressed to avoid your e-mail going unanswered for an extended period of time.

Cell Phones

- Turn cell phones off in meetings, restaurants, movies and churches. Turn to vibrating signal for a call you can't miss.
- Advise other participants before a meeting starts that you are expecting a call you must handle immediately. When the call comes in (vibrating signal), excuse yourself and handle it quickly. When you return to the meeting, thank them and turn off the phone.
- Use your cell phone discreetly on airplanes and turn it off when asked. Talk softly to avoid disturbing others. When you land and are instructed that you can use your cell phone, do not go into "cell yell" mode. Talk softly, a quick conversation to advise someone on the arrival and gate is sufficient.
- If you must make a phone call in a busy place, walk to a less crowded area. People do not want or need to hear your conversations.
- If you must use your cell phone in the car, it would be considerate to pull over and stop to make or receive a call, or purchase hands-free accessories so you do not have to take your hands off the wheel. In some states, it is now illegal to use cell phones while driving without a hands-free devise. Remember the safety of other people on the road while you are using your cell phone.
- If you place a call and are disconnected, it is your responsibility to call the person back immediately. Regardless of who is having the problem, if you placed the call you return it.
- Try to avoid asking to borrow someone's cell phone, but if you must, keep the call brief.

- Keep your conversations PG. Your use of the language might not be appropriate to the people around you, especially children.
- If someone is talking on their phone loud or using inappropriate language, it is better not to confront them. Have the manager of the restaurant, movie theater or venues approach them.

Phones

- Answer properly. Don't anticipate someone to be calling. Always treat the phone call as if it could be your boss or the chairman of the board on the line.
- Announce your full name when you answer. Speak clearly and slowly.
- Give the person on the line your undivided attention. Avoid eating, drinking, typing, printing or sending faxes while using the phone. Others can hear you and you need to be focused on your call.
- Change your voice mail when you are traveling, have meetings or will be out of the office for an extended period of time. Leave a number where you can be reached if necessary or a back-up contact.
- Leave exact messages on a voice mail to those you call (why you are calling, what you need/want and even a good time to call you back). Leave your full name, company name and title (if necessary), the time and day you are calling. Say your phone number clearly and slowly twice. Leave your phone number even if you call the person regularly. They may not have your number handy. It is always good to state the number in the beginning of the conversation with your name and again before you hang up. Say each number individually. Do not combine as five hundred and

fifty-five, twenty-two, twenty-two. It should be 5-5-5, 2-2-2-2.

- You should always include your area code.
- Follow through on all phone requests as soon as possible.
- Be conscious of the time you call and leave a message, particularly with international communications or virtual/home offices.
- Twenty-four hours return time of phone calls is appropriate and appreciated.

Speaker Phones/Conference Calls

- Be very careful how and when you use a speaker phone.
- Do not answer on the speaker phone. Once on a call, if you need to switch to the speaker phone, explain why and ask if the person on the other line would mind.
- Your business conversations should be one-on-one and not broadcast through the office. Use your speaker phone discreetly.
- Identify everyone in the room who will be participating in the conference call.
- When you speak, move closer to the phone and make sure only one person is speaking at a time.
- Make sure that your phone has the capacity to initiate a conference call and the designed number of callers.
- Identify yourself every time when you begin to speak if others are not familiar with you or your voice. Don't let a person on the other line guess who is speaking. They may miss part of the issue because they are trying to determine who is making the statement.

- Do not have side conversations during your conference call. They can be very disrupting and make it difficult to hear.
- Indicate to your listeners if you have to leave during the call and if you will be returning.
- If you are in charge of the call provide an agenda and keep the conversation moving in the designated time frame that was outlined. Have necessary follow-up to the call.
- Do not place the callers on hold if you must leave the call temporarily. Just place the phone down and identify yourself when you return to the call.

Voice Mail/Answering Machines

- Don't leave a message that rambles or gives numerous instructions. State the facts briefly, but be sure to provide enough information.
- Include your first and last name, company name and your title (if the person you are calling is not familiar with you). Don't assume everyone will know or remember you.
- Give the reason for your call and your full telephone number. Speak slowly and clearly and repeat the number. You can leave your phone number in the beginning and end of message or twice at the end. Most importantly, say it slowly.
- Never leave an important message, e.g., change of a meeting or location, without following up to confirm it was received.
- Never leave vague, mysterious or teasing messages. They could be misinterpreted and could lead to embarrassment or the wrong impression. You want to convey professionalism in all business dealings.

- Don't call back repeatedly to leave the same message if the person has not returned your call.
- In your office, don't choose an answering system that allows people to leave only very short messages. It is annoying and expensive to have to make repeated calls to an answering machine.
- Leave a businesslike greeting on your line. Be enthusiastic, but avoid jokes, weird music or cute sayings.
- On your machine, ask those calling to leave their name, company, response number, the time they called and a brief message.
- Provide callers with information about when you will return to the office, a back-up person or number to call and any other brief information deemed necessary.
- Smile when you are leaving the greeting on your own voice mail machine. It makes your tone friendlier.

Fax and Copy Machines

- Be courteous. Don't monopolize printers, copiers or fax machines.
- Sending an unsolicited 20-page document may tie up the receiver's fax line. Ask clients if they would prefer to have a long document mailed or faxed at night.
- Don't forward junk faxes, jokes, personal or sensitive information by fax. Other people could see it before it reaches the recipient.
- Faxes are not appropriate for all communications. Write your personal notes, invitations, thank-you notes, congratulations or condolences on good stationery or printed cards.
- Be conscious of the hour of the night or morning that a

fax is sent, especially when dealing with international communications or virtual/home offices.

- Always include a fax cover sheet that includes your full name, fax number, phone and address. Make it easy for the recipient to respond to you. Also include the number of pages being sent, including the cover sheet.

Laptops/Notebooks

- Be careful when traveling with a laptop. It is tempting for thieves.
- Because of security issues, your laptop must be sent through the airport security in a separate bin on the conveyor belt rather than carrying it through the metal detector.
- I highly recommend that you put a small label on your laptop. You may send it through the security belt at the airport and then be delayed passing through security. Laptops can be like a black suitcase going around the conveyer belt, and they all look the same. Your name and company would be sufficient for identification.
- If you use your laptop in flight, consider the people beside and in front of you. Do they want to sleep and you are constantly clicking the keys? That constant pounding can be extremely annoying. Shut it down and rest a bit or read a book.

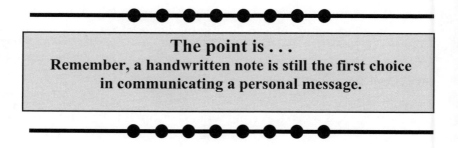

The point is . . .
Remember, a handwritten note is still the first choice
in communicating a personal message.

THREE

Behaving Professionally in the Workplace

Your office behavior affects how seriously you are taken by your supervisor and can affect your progress within your department and the organization. These brief thoughts about office behavior are good advice for someone beginning a career, but it is never too late to start acting more professionally even if you have been in the workplace for years. Review these points and resolve to correct and make the best out of your professional workplace.

Personal Matters

- In the morning, start work at the designated time. This does not mean after a 15-minute breakfast in the break room or at your desk. Eat breakfast at home or come in a few minutes early if you need to have your meal in the office kitchen or break room.
- Because labor laws require breaks throughout the work day, it is best to leave your work area for breaks and lunch. If you are asked to work through lunch, still make it a point to get away from your desk to at least walk around the office or to stretch. Your working capacity is only as good as your well being. It is documented by the Organization for Economic Cooperation and Development that an American worker annually works 1,804 hours, which is 300 to 400 hours more than workers in Europe. We are a driven nation of hard workers but we still need to take a break, a vacation or just a long weekend. If not, absence from work due to illness or just burn out will occur.

- As much as possible, avoid initiating or receiving personal phone calls or e-mail on company time. If you receive a personal call, give it three to five minutes. Then tell the caller you have to get back to work and offer to return the call during lunch, on your break or after work hours.
- If your company provides a cell phone to you don't abuse it. Watch your long distance personal calls and running up the bill by exceeding allotted minutes. Most phone plans offer free long distance and no limits on minutes. Just remember it was intended to be used for office business.
- Avoid creating or repeating office gossip, whether it concerns business or personal matters.
- Always show respect and professionalism for co-workers. You will not always agree with people's views but consider their views and how you could expand on their programs and ideas and offer your suggestions. Teamwork is what makes the office environment strong and morale increase.
- Respect the space of co-workers.
  - Avoid reading a co-worker's computer screen. You don't know what they are working on and it really isn't your business. Even if you are working on a project as a team, you still should wait to be invited to review their work.
  - Don't randomly just walk around the office and take tablets, pens, sticky notes or any other office supplies. Don't be known as the "office bandit." It is not a good brand for you.
  - Be quiet. Don't be screaming two doors down to see what another co-worker might want to do for lunch or after work. Either get up and walk to their desk (think of it as good exercise and a nice time to stretch) or call them on the phone to

ask. What if a customer were walking down the hall with your CEO and you were screaming to an office neighbor to go get a beer after work? It would surely not impress the customer.

o If you do overhear your office neighbors during their meeting or on the phone, don't become part of the conversation by answering some of their questions or offering your own opinions. If you were to be a part of that phone conversation or meeting, they would have invited you.

o If you are part of a conference call, then move to a conference area. People tend to talk louder when on a speaker phone and it could be very disruptive to everyone in the area. Move to a conference room to have a conference call and close the door. You might need a little pre-planning to reserve the room but it is worth it and will save on aggravation of all around you.

Work Responsibilities

- If you are given a responsibility, assume charge of the task. If it appears that time will not allow you to handle or complete the job, advise your supervisor of the situation as soon as you realize it and request more time or negotiate an acceptable solution.
- Give updates and status reports to your supervisor when you are working on a project. Don't wait for your supervisor to follow up. Don't let the supervisor assume you understand the job or think the job is being handled if you are encountering difficulties.
- Become involved in your staff meetings. Make sure you

have the agenda in advance and come prepared for the meeting. Arrive on time or three to five minutes early to get a good seat if seats are not assigned. If you have an opinion, express it. Don't complain but offer suggestions and good solutions. Be ready if you do get called upon for your opinion or thoughts. Play an important role in the development of your company and do not sit behind and offer your two cents under your breath.

- If you make a mistake, take responsibility, admit the problem and then move on. Don't pass the buck or make excuses.
- Never say, "It is not my job" or "It is not my responsibility." As a member of a team, you should share responsibilities. If you don't know an answer, admit it but search for the answer and then respond. Make it your job. And respond quickly.

Office Etiquette for Meetings Held in Your Office or Workplace

- You need to decide if it is more appropriate for you to meet your customers in the lobby or reception area or to have them escorted to your office. If the customer does arrive in your office for a meeting, then move around from your desk to shake hands. Avoid shaking hands over your desk or a table. The same "table shake" applies in a restaurant. At times it is unavoidable, but if possible always move around to make the distance more comfortable instead of stretching and shaking.
- Offer them a seat and it is appropriate to have a little chit-chat prior to the start of the meeting. Make sure in the process of the information that you gather over the

course of working with a customer that you have a little personal information, but not too personal. It could be the soccer game for their children, a cruise they just went on to celebrate their anniversary or the home they just purchased. Something that would set the pace for a good start to the business portion of the meeting. But don't spend so much time on asking personal questions that they pull out their phone camera and show you a video of the entire soccer game. That's way too much chit-chat.

- It is appropriate to offer refreshments or to have them already set and ready to go for the meeting.
- Have your materials ready.   This could include a PowerPoint presentation ready on your laptop, printed materials or any other information necessary to conduct a meeting.
- Know when to leave or end the meeting. Present your case and then end it. End on a high so they want to come back for more.
- Always follow up within 24 hours if possible. Some information could take months but immediate requests should be handled with quick attention. That will set the stage and show your interest and involvement with the case, program or project.

More Hints for the Office

- Remember that a client could phone or come into the office at any time. Be aware that your behavior or conversations may be subject to scrutiny by clients as well as by your supervisor/employer.
- No alcoholic beverages should be consumed during a luncheon and minimal consumption is wise during an

evening function. Exceeding the legal limit for alcohol is grounds for dismissal from most companies. Remember, if you attend a business function, you represent your company and should always follow company policies.

- If food is brought or sent to your office by a supplier, vendor or customer, share it. Take a portion and then place it where all members of the company may enjoy it. If a gift comes to a specific department, it is still good to share with other staff. If food remains at the end of the day, it can be taken home.
- Be a positive problem-solver. If you detect an operations problem, don't point it out without offering a few suggestions for a solution.

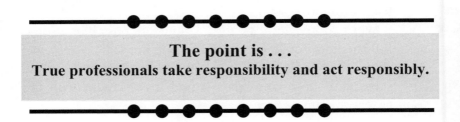

The point is . . .
True professionals take responsibility and act responsibly.

FOUR

Connecting and Getting the Best End Results

Receptions, association luncheons and other networking events are occasions to meet new people and make contacts that may lead to potential clients. But if you spend the time with friends, focus on the buffet or bar and leave without accomplishing some business goals, you've failed to take advantage of great opportunities. Your goal should be to meet people, exchange business cards and perhaps pave the way for future contacts or meetings. It is not appropriate to use receptions or networking events to present a proposal or contract or to conduct a business meeting. Avoid entering the room with a cart on wheels full of brochures. This is your time to set up a meeting not conduct one. Make these events the ideal time to connect and start a solid business relationship or renew a lost or forgotten piece of business.

Attitude

For some people, entering a room full of strangers is easy, but for others it is pure torture. Your attitude plays a major role when you attend a reception or any business function. You can enter a room with any of the following attitudes:

- There is nobody interesting to talk to here.
- I'd rather be in my hotel room watching television.
- I'm here to party and eat and drink as much as I can and not to network and connect with people and new companies.

- I am shy, fear meeting strangers, feel uncomfortable and awkward and lack self-confidence.
- Or, I'm here to meet as many people as I can and hope to find some future business.

Both introverts and extroverts attend business and social gatherings. You need to find the group that fits you best. But your ultimate goal is to mix with all groups.

The Basic Steps

- Enter the room with your head held high and tell yourself you can do it.
- Look for two or three people together and approach them.
- Start with a good, solid handshake.
- Look each person straight in the eyes as you introduce yourself.
- Listen carefully to their names. Repeat their names and then try to use them again during your conversation. Repeating the names will help you remember them, but don't overdo it by saying their name in every sentence. A little is enough.
- Turn your body toward the person you are meeting. Do not be distracted or look all around the room for other people to meet. Give the person speaking your undivided attention. Be attentive and listen to what that person is saying.
- Exchange business cards. Always have plenty of them and have them ready to hand out. (See business card exchange, Chapter Five).
- Eventually, excuse yourself and move on to other people.

Conversation Tips

- A little chit-chat is good in the beginning. Easy topics include names, hometown and work. Even talk about the weather, traveling to the event, upcoming events, or any safe and easy talk. Perhaps you'll find a commonality.
- Your best information for chit-chat comes from exchanging business cards. Once you receive a business card, review it. Use it to ask questions, their title, company, office address, degree or certification all are great topics for communication.
- Avoid controversial topics including politics, religion or personal questions.
- Reading the local paper or national papers daily to stay up-to-date with daily events and the news always helps make conversation easy.
- Pick up cues from name badges if people are wearing them.
- Be proactive; initiate conversation rather than waiting. Ask open-ended questions.
- Include everyone in your conversation.
- Stick to familiar topics to help you feel at ease.
- Respond to comments and questions of others.
- Don't monopolize the conversation.
- Don't gossip. Don't talk about people.
- Don't get on a soapbox, teach, preach or attempt to impress.
- Don't continue a conversation if the other person is obviously bored or not responding. Yawning would be a good cue to end a conversation and move on to the next person.
- Remember to listen attentively.

How to Move On

- Since the goal should be to work the room, do not get trapped in one conversation all evening.
- Thank the others for the conversation, express pleasure in meeting them or use another appropriate transition to depart. End with a handshake and move on to meet other people.
- You may mention getting something to eat or drink or needing to find another person before the event ends. Just be careful because they may want to join you for that drink or food.
- Excuse yourself graciously and promise to respond or to anticipate a response if future contact was requested or promised.
- If all else fails, take them to another person that you know. Introduce them with a little explanation about both of them and then move on.

Making the Most by Connecting at Receptions

- If a reception is held in your own company, where you know a lot of the employees, you should meet people outside your department whom you may just pass in the hallway. If a seated dinner follows the reception, do not sit with your fellow workers. Move to a different department's table.
- The reception may be during an industry convention or meeting. Circulate out of your comfort zone and meet new people. Don't stay with co-workers and friends. Set a goal of how many new people you will meet that evening. Make it a fun adventure.

- If the reception occurs during your first time at a group meeting, at a new church or at a new venue, make the most of it. Go into the reception with a great attitude and meet as many people as you can.
- Don't hide. Don't go to the rest room or to a corner of a room and simply observe. Be an active participant.
- Don't go immediately to the food area and put a plate in your hand, and don't go to the bar area and hang out there all evening. It is difficult to shake hands and meet someone when you have a plate in one hand and a drink in the other. Mingle, work the room and then get something to eat and drink.

Pre-event Planning

- Do your homework. Find out who is attending and what you may need to know when you meet these people.
- Review the attendee list before going to the reception. The list may be a part of your registration packet at the convention or you may need to call the company and request a list.
- Be organized. Go prepared with business cards. Keep them where they can be reached easily to present to your new contacts. A good hint is to wear a jacket with pockets. Keep your cards in the right pocket and put contacts cards in the left (or switch if you are left handed).
- Know why you are there. Are you looking for business, trying to meet specific people, networking and meeting everyone possible to increase your visibility, going in

place of your boss to represent your company or just taking advantage of the free food and drink?

- If it is a reception and a trade show, you can send out pre-event post cards, flyers, notes or letters to all attendees. Let them know a little about your company, where your booth will be located and your promotions. A prize or drawing usually will bring more people to your booth. Just make sure they are mailed in plenty of time. There is nothing worse than to have your pre-mailer arrive after the event.

- If the function is for a smaller group of people, you can call them before the networking opportunity and see if they could meet you there. Ask for a specific, short period of time. Make sure you are available at that time, be prepared, set up a future time to meet, end with a handshake, thank them for their time and then move on.

- Remember, a reception is a time to exchange cards and set up future meetings, not to conduct business. But at a trade show, you can discuss business and maybe even close a deal.

Tips for Trade Show Exhibitors

- Before the trade show, send out mailers with your booth number (if available) and information about your give-aways or games. Make sure attendees receive your mailer in plenty of time to schedule your booth into their plans.

- Try to get a good location for your booth. Or try to get a position next to a popular location or the food area.

- Make your booth area approachable. Don't stand behind a table or sit in a chair.
- Many exhibitors now dress in golf shirts with company logos or similar outfits, depending on their product or market. Casual clothes and comfortable shoes are appropriate for the long hours spent on trade show floors. But make sure that the "casual" appearance is appropriate for the trade show, your perception and brand. If not, then you might need to suffer with a coat and tie or low to medium heels.
- Greet everyone and invite them into your booth area.
- Have give-aways, games or gimmicks.
- Know the difference between a prospect, someone just browsing and someone stopping for your gift or food.
- Respond immediately to any requests made by possible clients.

Tips for Trade Show Attendees

- Do your homework and be prepared when you enter the trade show floor.
- Set measurable, specific goals that fit your business strategies and help you stay focused and on track.
- Know whom you want to meet and plan your strategy to meet everyone within the given time of the trade show.
- Be sure to carry a good supply of business cards so you won't run out midway into a meeting or a trade show, and don't leave your cards in your car or hotel room.

- Don't be cheap at trade shows. If you don't buy a booth, then don't be walking up and down the aisles selling your product. Selling from the aisle is not ethical.
- Don't circulate with friends and socialize when you should be making new contacts and creating business opportunities.
- Make the best use of your energies and talents by planning appointments with vendors when you are fresh and not overly tired.
- Keep files of materials gathered at trade shows so you have ready access to vendors' information.
- Follow up after the show to ensure you have all the information you need.

Follow up

- Immediately upon returning to your office, send a handwritten note to every potential client you met. Even better, carry note cards with you and write them from the trade show or meeting site at the end of each day.
- Follow up any request within 24 to 48 hours. Don't let contacts' business cards stack up. Make the phone calls you need to make and file or enter into your database the contact information you need for future use.
- It takes only three minutes to write a thank-you note and address the envelope. Those three minutes can make a great impression on a client or potential client.

- Be careful about e-mail responses. If you are simply sending requested information, then e-mail is appropriate. Never send an e-mail in place of a handwritten thank-you note.
- Be as good as your word. If you promised to send something, research something or do something for a client, then do it! And do it as soon as possible.
- Does the person's request need a phone call? If so, do your research and respond quickly. Should you leave a voice mail if the client is not available? Yes, but tell the client a good time to reach you or when you will try again.
- Your Web site can be a starting point for clients. Print your Web address on your business cards.

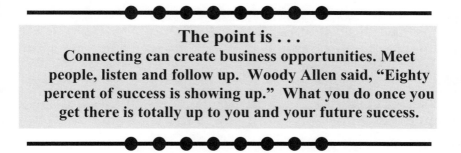

The point is . . .

Connecting can create business opportunities. Meet people, listen and follow up. Woody Allen said, "Eighty percent of success is showing up." What you do once you get there is totally up to you and your future success.

FIVE

Handshakes, Introductions and Thank-You Notes

First impressions can be as easy as a smile, your handshake or a proper introduction. To create a lasting impression would be a thank-you note for a lunch with a prospective client, a dinner with the boss or a thank-you to an associate for a job well done.

The Handshake

You can make several mistakes with something as easy as a handshake. Men will think they need to give women a wimpy handshake so not to hurt them, and a woman feels she needs to give a bone-crushing shake to a man to show her power. People hesitate to shake hands with clients or acquaintances possibly because of their gender, ethnic background or age. Should you bow with an international visitor or shake hands? So let's end some of these myths.

- Greet a person, no matter their age, size, gender or nationality, with a nice smile and good eye contact.
- Extend your hand and offer a nice firm, web-to-web handshake. No need to bring me to my knees with the shake but a firm, solid shake will do. Yes, some countries' greetings will vary, but generally all business people are accustomed to the Westernized handshake. If you are in doubt in certain countries, then pause an allow them to offer their hand first. They may not so do not extend yours.

- The handshake should be two shakes or a few seconds. No need to hang on during your whole conversation.
- Be in a good stance with the other person. Face them directly with your shoulders facing theirs, feet squarely planted on the ground and your heart aiming toward their heart. The main purpose of this position is to be sure you are focused on that person. Don't be looking around them or over their head to see who you need to meet next. Give that person a concentrated effort and you might even remember their name. In the United States we stand approximately 2 ½ to 3 feet from other people. That seems to be our comfort zone. But in other countries, some will be inches away from you while others prefer a greater distance. Whichever the case, do not try to get closer to them nor step back if they are too close. Some may also place a hand on you during the entire conversation. Just ignore it.
- When they say their name to you, repeat it. You don't have to repeat a name over and over during your conversation.
- If you forget their name ask them. Don't miss out on the conversation with them because you are just thinking of how you know them and their name. You might say, "I am so sorry I just cannot remember your name." Or "please help me and tell me your name again." Try to avoid asking them this question every time you see them. You might want to try a little name association or just write it down if you know you will see them at an upcoming luncheon or meeting.
- Be aware of the double handshake person. Some people will grab on with both hands. Be prepared because they may hold on for the entire conversation Try to concentrate on what they are saying instead of releasing the grip. The best suggestion is to ask that person a question that

requires more than a yes or no answer. Hopefully they have to think about it a little and will let go slightly on their grip. This is your opportunity to get out of the hold. You only have a second to do this so react quickly. If not, you are in their power until the end of your conversation.

- I say a handshake is worth risking germs. Carry a hand sanitizer and after you walk away get it out and apply in abundance. There are more germs on the door you will be exiting than on the person's hand you just shook. Plus it is tough to tell them you don't want to shake their hand because you heard them coughing or saw them blowing their nose. Hopefully they will not offer their hand to you if they are spreading germs.

- If you live in an area of colder weather or are wearing a pair of gloves, it is much nicer to remove them before shaking hands. It can be done quickly without any great fuss. If you are skiing and on the slopes and all dressed up in your ski outfit, it is appropriate to leave your gloves or mittens on.

- Many people are very comfortable with exchanging hugs and kisses. Be prepared. A person may extend their hand to you but then pull you in for the hug, possibly even a kiss and a pat on the back. Even if it makes you uncomfortable, it is over quickly. It is always nice to reciprocate. Be prepared for the international kiss and hug. They usually last a little longer and could be two or three kisses. Aim for right cheeks first and try not to hit noses or bump heads. If you are traveling to another country or dealing with a person from another country, research and understand their customs and traditions. It is always nice to be prepared and they will appreciate your extra effort to respect them. Most countries have adopted the universal handshake into their customs for business.

- Start and end your conversations with a handshake. Remember all the points of good eye contact, the smile and your stance. A last impression is as important as your first.

Name Badges

The sheriff's badge was worn over their heart to protect them from gunfire, so the tradition started with the name badge being worn on the left. But over the years the tradition has changed. I recommend wearing your name badge on the right so as people lean in to shake your hand, the eye will go directly to the name on the right. But the argument to this suggestion is that you should wear your badge on the left so as people pass by they can look and read your name badge. So I guess the choice is up to you and what you feel would be better in your connecting situations.

If you need to print your own name badge, do it in large, easy-to-read letters. Men, I know the pocket of your jacket is on the left so you have a tendency to attach the name badge to your pocket, try to get into the habit of using your right lapel instead. It looks just as good and may even lay a little better and flatter.

If your name badge is attached to a lanyard, make sure you adjust the length so others are not reading your belly button or your chest. Find a spot so people see it quickly when you are meeting them. Remove your name badge for photos and speeches.

Business Cards

There is a proper exchange of business cards and it is not throwing them across a table or desk. Many countries feel that Americans are not formal in many of our business practices and leading the list is the exchange of business cards. The Japanese "meishi kokan" or business card exchange is an extension of your organization and shows respect and a critical first impression. The "meishi" (business card) is handled in a way to show respect and professionalism. Stand to present your cards and present and receive the cards with both hands. Present with your name facing the person that will receive the card. Just hold the card in the corners so you are not covering your name or important information on the card. As you are handing the card execute a slight bow. If dealing with other countries, it is recommended that you have one side of your card in English and the other side in their language. When you present, hand the card to the person with their language side up.

Once you receive another person's card, take the time to read it completely. This provides information for further discussion and also shows respect and interest. In a meeting, you do not need to immediately put the cards away but can line the cards up on a desk or table to remember the names and further references. Remember to use the family name of your counterpart when dealing internationally. We are very informal in the United States, even at a first meeting calling people by their first names. In other countries this is not acceptable.

Business cards generally are written horizontally and measure 3 ½ by 2 inches. Creativity is great but do not be so creative that the card is confusing. Provide your name with no honorifics, your title, company and full address. Then list the phone number or numbers to reach you including the office, fax and if you wish your cell phone. Include your e-mail address and Web site. Don't make it difficult for people to contact you.

Business Card Tips

- Always have plenty. Never leave home or the office without them. If I attend a large conference and ask someone for their card and their response is, "I am so sorry but I ran out" or "I forgot to bring them," I question how professional or serious are they about their business. This may be your only opportunity to leave behind your name or company information.

- Keep them in a business card case and easy to reach. Don't fumble in your pockets or briefcase looking for them. Make it easy and professional to distribute them.

- Make sure the cards are up-to-date. Never cross out your old e-mail address, phone number or a co-worker's name and then write on the card and give it to a person. Now you can easily make cards on your computer so there is no excuse.

- Never pull out your business card from your wallet that has been in your hip pocket.

- Do not write on another person's business card. It shows disrespect for the "gift" that they just presented to you.

- A business card is not your life history. Keep them easy to read with large enough print. But be aware that additional information, such as degrees, may need to be added if you are dealing globally.

- If you are dealing internationally, be aware of colors and symbols that may be offensive.

- During a trade show or a meeting when you are exchanging many cards, keep your business cards in one area and then store the ones you receive in another. Don't pull out a stack of cards that are a combination of yours and those of others and shuffle through them to hand out yours.

- For social purposes, do not include your business card. Never include your business card in a Christmas card or holiday card. This is a time to share well wishes, not to book another piece of business.
- Of course there are exceptions to every rule but think professional and respectful in your business card exchanges.

Introductions – "HOW"

Introductions can be confusing. Who should you introduce first and what exactly should you say when introducing someone. My "HOW" system seems to work well in remembering the protocol of introductions. "HOW" stands for Higher, Older, Woman.

The lower-ranking person is introduced to the higher-ranking person.
"Ms. President, I would like to introduce Mr. Vice President." (Higher-ranking person's name first)

The younger person is introduced to the older person.
"Mr. Lott, I would like for you to meet my grandson, Shaeffer." (Older person's name first)

The man is introduced to a woman.
"Mrs. Albert, I would like for you to meet Mr. Ross." (Woman's name first)

Of course there are always exceptions but this is always a good starting point. Just remember that generally rank is considered first in introductions.

Exceptions:
- The head of a country, royal family, church official, high political positions like the governor or president are always shown respect and introduced first.
- A client should be introduced first even if the President of the company is of a higher rank or senior in age. It just shows respect to that client in hopes of future business.

Avoid long, flowery introductions: "This is my beautiful, wonderful and darling wife." Just "I would like for you to meet my wife, Evelyn," is sufficient.

The proper introductions for the heads of state or minister, ambassador or senior church official is to use "His/Her Excellency." In the British Commonwealth, the preferred introduction is "The Right Honourable." "Madame" or "Mister" precedes titles in the United States as in "Mr. President." Addressing these officials in person use "Mr. Ambassador," "Madame Ambassador," "Excellency" or "Sir."

Forgetting a Name

If you can't remember a person's name and then another person joins you, the easiest way to handle it is to say, "Have you met Sutton Gary?" Then you hope that your nameless friend will come back and introduce himself by saying his name. If they don't then Sutton can say, "I am so sorry but I didn't catch your name." But, of course, Sutton could make matters worse when she turns to you and says "I am sorry, you didn't tell me your friend's name." Then, unfortunately, you have to face facts and admit you forgot his name. It happens to all of us.

Make it easy if you have not seen a person in an extended period of time. Just walk up to her, extend your hand and say, "Hello, I'm Kristan Gallo and we met at the last conference in New Orleans." Hopefully the other person will return the greeting with her name.

Co-Workers Helping with the Name Game

If you are with a co-worker or in a social situation with your partner, an easy way to help with introductions is the "nameless game." If I am with my husband and he cannot remember the person that is approaching us, he will say, "I would like for you to meet my wife." My name is not mentioned nor does he make any effort to search out their name. That is my cue that he cannot remember the person's name so I immediately extend my hand and say, "Hello, I'm Colleen and very nice to meet you." Generally, they will come back and say their name but not always. It is a great practice that usually works. You can always substitute with "co-worker," "son," "daughter" or "associate." You may not get the other person's name but it does help to avoid embarrassment.

Table Introductions

Don't sit at a luncheon for an hour or longer having no idea who is seated across from you. When you enter a luncheon or any meal function, when you don't know everyone at the table, make an effort to go around the table and introduce yourself to everyone seated. It starts off the conversation much better and also gives you the opportunity to meet eight or nine new people. Don't wait for a business card exchange at the table to be your first opportunity to meet them. Use every opportunity possible.

Group Introductions

If you are in a situation at a reception talking to a group of people and a person that you know comes up to the group, it is your responsibility to introduce them to everyone. But if you cannot remember a few names, then the best method is to introduce the new person and then ask everyone to go around and introduce themselves to the new person. It works well and then you know all the names.

Thank-You Notes "3-3-3"

Thank-you notes are becoming a part of the past and shame on us. The handwritten note is still and should be a very critical part of both our social and business interactions. Technology has made it too easy to just jot down a quick thank-you via an e-mail. In some cases this is acceptable but in most cases it is not.

If a person sends you flowers for a job you just completed or they are thanking you for a great project, yes, you need to send them a thank-you note for their thank-you. I am sure you are wondering when the "thank-you" should end. But if some one sends you a gift as a thank-you for a job you have just done for them, this is one time a phone call or an e-mail is accepted and appreciated. You are just alerting them that their gift arrived. You can still follow up with a handwritten note to complete the cycle.

No, you should not send e-mail thank you notes or any other form of "quick" thank-you that you might consider for wedding gifts, high school or college graduation gifts That is very lazy and disrespectful.

I promise thank-you notes do not take long and they are not painful. I created my "3-3-3" system to make it quick and easy.

Everyone should have thank-you notes available for both personal use and business. There are many types and you should

select the ones that match your personality. For business keep them professional and in good taste. A single card or fold-over will work.

"3-3-3"

- Keep your cards in an easy location so they can be reached quickly. Have an ample supply.
- The first "3" is for three minutes. It should take you only three minutes to write your card. That even includes getting the card, the mailing address and then writing the card.
- The second "3" is for three lines. You need only three lines in a thank-you note. It doesn't need to be long but always mention the gift, how you might use it and then end with how you hope to work with them again in the future, spend time with them or an appropriate closing.
- The last "3" is for three days. Try really hard to send out your thank-you notes within three days after you receive the gift. Try to not reach the three-week or three-month time period.
- It generally is not necessary or appropriate to include your business card. Business cards are usually included in the beginning of the working relationship.

Sample Thank You Note:

Dear Marc,
Thank you so much for the beautiful flowers that just arrived.
They are providing such a great addition to my office. I enjoyed
working with you on the marketing project and am looking
forward to future opportunities together.

My best,
Judi

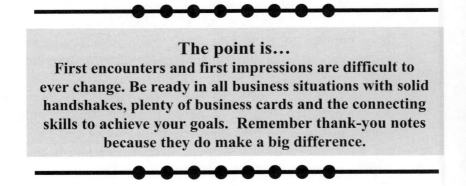

The point is...
**First encounters and first impressions are difficult to
ever change. Be ready in all business situations with solid
handshakes, plenty of business cards and the connecting
skills to achieve your goals. Remember thank-you notes
because they do make a big difference.**

SIX

Dining and Table Etiquette

Granted, growing up in a fast-food world does not provide many opportunities for learning the finer points of dining etiquette. But in a business setting, minding your manners can make a lasting impression. The tips in this chapter provide the basics about what you should and should not do in a business/formal setting. The following four chapters will help you negotiate a complex table setting and give advice about hosting a business dinner and being on your best behavior at other meal functions.

Setting the Table

Simple dinner meals
- Knives and spoons are on the right. An old trick is that knife and spoon both have five letters and so does right. I have provided a little more explanation below and other tricks on navigating the table and all its many parts.
- Forks and napkins are on the left (except for the cocktail fork that is on the far right). The same old trick that fork has four letters and so does left.
- Glassware/crystal is on the right.
- Coffee cup and saucer are on the right or are placed before or during dessert.
- Plates, such as a salad plate or bread and butter plate, are on the left.
- No matter if you are right- or left-handed, you cannot move these pieces around to suit your comfort and ease of eating and drinking. Where they are set is where they must stay.

Elaborate dining

- Usually replace the flatware and china before each course.
- Dessert utensils are placed horizontally above the dinner plate. The dessert spoon (bowl facing left) goes above the fork (tines facing right). Move these utensils into position on both sides of the plate before you start to eat. Receiving both utensils allows you to use either one or both for your dessert. Just a little trick . . . start with the fork on the left and the spoon on the right. Then just slide them to the horizontal pattern above the plate.

Styles of Eating

American: An inefficient style of eating/dining but common in the United States. You cut, place the knife on the top of your plate with the blade facing the center of the plate, switch hands with the fork, scoop the food up and eat. In a formal setting, cut one bite at a time; at other times, cut two or three pieces at the most.

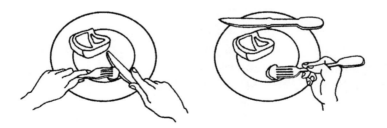

Continental/European: Much easier and more sophisticated style of eating. The knife remains in the left hand and the fork in the right. Only one bite is cut at a time.

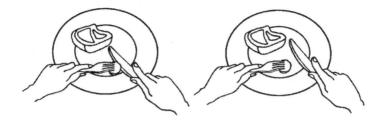

Dining Rules to Live By

- **Silverware:** The rule to remember is once you pick up any piece of your silverware, it never touches the table again. Don't let your silverware rest partially on the table and partially on your plate. Place the blade of the knife, the tines of the fork or the bowl of the spoon facing the 10 if looking at the face of a clock. The bottom of the silverware will be at the four position. In most cases, work from the outside in with your silverware.

- **The "b" and "d" rule or BMW:** To get your bearings when you are seated, think BMW—bread, meal, water. Your bread, meal and water go left to right, just like the letters. Some people remember "b" for bread and "d" for drink. Note that the lower case letter "b" on your left hand facing the plate stands for bread and the lower case "d" on your right hand facing the plate stands for drink. Make these letters by putting your index finger up in the air and then making a circle with your thumb and middle finger. The "d" sign is the actual "d" used in sign language.

51

- **Hosts:** Take your cues from them. This includes where they may ask you to sit, when to place your napkin on your lap, when to start the meal, making toasts, discussing business, keeping pace with them while they are eating (if you need to slow down or speed up) and when to finish the meal, time to leave and place the napkin on the table.

- **When to start to eat:** Wait until everyone is served. If there are hosts, they either will start to eat or will make a gesture or comment for guests to enjoy the meal. When the host begins, you may also start. If a person at your table has requested a special meal, he should instruct everyone else at the table to begin, since his meal may be delayed. Feel free to begin your meal. If the person with the special meal just sits there and does not advise everyone to start, the host may offer to check with the wait staff regarding the status of the meal. If they still do not encourage you to start your meal, you may ask if you and your other guests should start so their meals do not get cold.

- **Napkin:** Place the napkin on your lap as soon as you are seated or wait for your host to place his on his lap and then follow immediately. Your napkin is not a flag to signal the start of a race, so don't flap it all around. Just place the unfolded napkin on your lap. If it is large, leave it only half open or in the triangle if folded that way. If your silverware is rolled into the napkin on the table at your setting, just take the entire napkin and place it on your lap and unroll it. Then place the silverware on the table in the correct positions. If you leave the table, place your napkin on the chair and gently push the chair back under the table. Some people have a problem with coming back and sitting where their napkin was placed. If that truly bothers you, you can always place it on the left arm of the chair, back of the chair or even to the left of your plate. At the end of the meal, pick up the napkin from the center and loosely place it on the table to the left of your plate. The napkin should stay on your lap until you actually get up to leave the dining area. If there is a speaker after your meal the napkin should remain on your lap. Never use the napkin as a hanky or tissue. If you sneeze, you can blot, but don't blow your nose or rub your face. Don't wipe your mouth with one hand while holding a knife or fork with the other.

- **Dropping something or using the wrong item**: If you drop a piece of your silverware or your napkin, let it go. You can either ask for another one or the wait staff will notice and replace it for you. If your neighbor happens to take your napkin or maybe your bread and butter plate or starts drinking your coffee, let it go. You can place your bread on your entrée plate or ask the waiter for another glass, napkin or silverware. Try to do all of this without drawing attention to the neighbor who just took all your utensils. Don't panic if you use the wrong piece of flatware. Just keep using it and ask the waiter for a replacement when you need it.

- **Double-dipping:** Never take a chip or hors d'oeuvre and dip it into a sauce or a dip, take a bite and then dip it again. Either break the piece of food in half so you can dip both pieces or just dip the initial piece. Or if possible, place some of the dip on your own plate. You still shouldn't double dip but at least you are not all sharing the same food.

- **Bread:** First place the butter on your plate. Do not go directly to the bread with the butter. Do not cut your bread but break it in half. Then break off only one bite-sized piece of bread at a time from the slice of bread or roll. Butter that piece, set the knife down on the plate and then eat that one piece. Do not butter the whole roll or slice of bread (or even half) and then just start to bite off pieces.

- **Salt and pepper:** Remember salt and pepper are married. They go together. Even if someone asks you to pass just the salt, pick up both the salt and pepper and pass them together. Place them on the table next to the person and then they can select what they wish. Do not hand them to the person making the request. When setting the table, place salt and pepper together at both ends of the table.

- **The squirting lemon:** Cup the lemon with your hand before you squeeze it into a drink or over your fish or meal. After you have squeezed the lemon, place it on the side of your plate or drop it into the drink. If the lemon is covered in a mesh, then just set it to the side of your plate.

- **The turnover:** If a coffee cup and saucer are placed at your setting, do not turn it upside down to signify you don't want coffee or tea. Allow the wait staff to ask you if you prefer not to have any. You can either tell them no thank you or just signal with your hand held over the cup that you do not wish them to pour coffee or tea for you. The wait staff may then turn your cup over to signify that you have been asked and refused or they may even take it away entirely. By turning over your cup, you could indicate to the wait team they already checked your table so they may not come to offer other people their choice of beverages. They have a system, so let them do it.

- **Sweetener packets:** Do not shake or flick packets. Place the empty packages under your iced tea plate, coffee saucer or entrée plate. A good wait staff will see them and take them away when they clear your plates. Other items like wrappers from crackers and straws or plastic creamer cups can be handled the same way, or just place them on the edge of your saucer or bread plate.

- **Lipstick and makeup:** Don't apply makeup at the table nor disappear under the table for a few seconds to put some on quickly. Just excuse yourself and go to the restroom to apply lipstick, lip gloss or any touch up if necessary during the meal.

- **Toothpicks:** My rule on toothpicks is 1½. You'd better be 1½ miles from all people before that toothpick ever goes in your mouth. It is not cool to be walking out a restaurant with a toothpick hanging out of your mouth.

Minding your Table Manners

- When you approach the table, enter your chair from the left. Purses, briefcases and all personal articles should stay off the table. Put them on the floor to your right or under your seat. If it is not a part of the meal or table setting, it should not be on the table during the meal. When you leave the table, exit to your right and pick up your belongings.
- Never chew with your mouth open, and no matter how urgent you think it is to talk, don't do it with your mouth

full. Wait gracefully.

- Always remember to sit up straight. You don't need to be at a 90-degree angle but also don't be at a 45-degree angle to your plate. Lean forward slightly to eat and then back again.
- Keep your elbows off the table. If you're in doubt about your hands, put them in your lap. Whether you are right- or left-handed, your arms and elbows should always stay close to you.
- Burping is so embarrassing, but if it happens, cover your mouth and just say, "Excuse me."
- Never pick your teeth at the table. If you have something in your teeth, take a drink of water and if that doesn't work, excuse yourself and go to the restroom.
- Don't ask questions. If someone at your table takes a pill, don't ask if they are sick or why they are taking it. If someone gets up to leave the table for whatever reason, again, make no comments.
- Watch your speed. Keep pace with everyone at your table. Remember the rule about following the pace of the host.
- When you have completed your meal, just leave your plate in front of you, don't push it away or move it. Don't be so relaxed that you tilt or push your chair back.
- Don't stack your plates when you are finished with your meal. Just leave them where they should be placed.
- Don't cover your plate with your napkin or roll up the paper napkin and place it on your plate. Leave the napkin on your lap until you are ready to leave the table. Then just place either the paper or linen napkin to the left of the plate.
- Don't hand your plate or plates to the wait staff. Allow them to do their job and pick them up in their own system. Respect fellow diners. Even if you are seated in

a restaurant's smoking section, always ask permission to smoke. Do not start to smoke while others are still eating and never use your plate as an ashtray.

- Try to postpone business discussions until the end of the meal if time will permit. Do not spread out all your papers over the table. A nice portfolio works best to keep everything organized and confined.

Some Hints about Food

- Always pass food to the right (also with business card exchanges).
- If your soup, coffee or any hot item has steam coming off the top, give it a few seconds to cool down. Don't blow on your food or drink.
- Don't salt or season your food before you taste it.
- Cut one bite of meat or food at a time in formal settings. In a less formal setting, you can cut two or three pieces at the most but it is a good habit to stick with one.
- Refrain from dunking anything in your soup, milk or coffee. Cookies, donuts or crackers should not be crumbled or dunked. Treat crackers like bread and break off one piece at a time, butter and eat.
- Items with handles should be passed with the handle toward the other person. It helps them accept the bowl or pitcher. If an item is too hot, set it next to the person or if the platter is heavy, you can offer to help hold it while they take their food off the platter. Then they can assist the person to their right.
- If a long-handled tea spoon is provided for iced tea, use it only to stir sugar or sweetener into the tea. If a small plate is provided with your iced tea, then place the spoon

on this small plate. If there is not a plate under your glass, then use your dinner plate, coffee cup saucer or bread and butter plate. If no plate is available, then rest the spoon on the blade of your knife. If no tea spoon is provided, use the other spoon at your place setting.

- If the entrée and the salad are served together, you may use the entrée fork for both. You don't have to keep switching back and forth between the two forks. Also, if a salad is the main course, then you can use the entrée fork. Again, it is pretty safe to start from the outside and work your way in with all your silverware.
- When in doubt, eat with a utensil, rather than with your fingers, even those foods that you may eat with your hands at home. Use a fork to cut French fries into bite-sized pieces unless they are served with a hamburger or sandwich, and then you can use your fingers. Eat bacon with a fork unless it is too crisp, then fingers are acceptable, too. Chicken, or any other meat at a business meal, is not finger food. You should use the knife and fork.
- If you don't know how to eat something that comes with your meal, leave it or watch to see how others eat it and follow their lead.
- If it's on your plate, it's meant to be eaten. So enjoy!

Soup Guidelines

- Lean forward slightly to eat the soup.
- Dip the spoon sideways into the soup, going away from you.
- Just skim the top of the soup, don't fill the spoon completely.
- Sip off the edge, not from the front of your spoon. Don't

put the whole spoon in your mouth. You take medicine from the front of a spoon and eat soup from the side.

- If you need that last spoonful, tilt the soup bowl away from you. Don't pick it up and drink it.
- If consomme or broth is served in a cup with one or two handles, you may pick up the soup cup and drink it. If there are two handles, hold both handles.
- Do not crumble crackers into your soup. Treat crackers like bread, one bite at a time. Rest the crackers on the dish under the soup plate.
- You may put several oyster crackers in the soup at a time. Leave the extra crackers on the dish under the soup plate.
- Don't blow on the soup. Let it cool and then eat.
- Both soup cups and soup plates should be served with a saucer or plate beneath them. When your soup is served in a soup cup, the spoon should lie on the saucer when not in use or when you have completed the soup. But when soup is served in a soup plate, the spoon is left in the soup plate instead of on the dish under it.

Wait Staff Interactions

- Wait staff are trained so let them do their job. Allow them to take your plate and clear the table. Don't stack your plates or hand them to the wait staff. An exception: If you are seated in a far corner or awkward place, then it may be appropriate to hand your plate to the waiter.
- Be considerate of waiters when they are serving a large setting for a convention or meal. Allow them to set all the meals before you make any special requests like extra dressing, another drink or hot tea instead of coffee.
- Courses are normally set from the left and removed from

the right. An easy way to remember is "remove" from "right." All drinks are served and removed from the right. It helps to know so you can sit back while the wait staff places or removes your dishes.

- If you need to get a waiter's attention, just raise your hand quietly. You do not need to get everyone's attention in the entire room by waving your hand frantically, signaling with your napkin or raising your voice.
- Remember, it takes only a second to turn to your waiter and say, "Thank you."

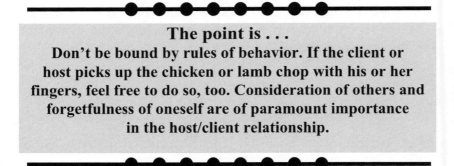

The point is . . .
Don't be bound by rules of behavior. If the client or host picks up the chicken or lamb chop with his or her fingers, feel free to do so, too. Consideration of others and forgetfulness of oneself are of paramount importance in the host/client relationship.

SEVEN

Negotiating the Tabletop

Your first encounter with multiple utensils and glasses does not have to be intimidating. Formal table settings are laid out logically. You need to remember only a few simple rules to be able to read the tabletop road map. This chapter gives course-by-course directions to get you to the end of the meal without a breakdown in your good manners.

Utensils

- There can be as many as three forks to the left of the service plate and three knives to the right. You should never find more than three of one utensil at a place setting.
- The only exceptions will be the butter knife that is placed on the bread plate and a fourth fork, the small oyster fork, which is placed at the extreme right of the place setting and is used for oysters or shrimp cocktail. Its tines should be resting in the bowl of the soup spoon.
- After the soup spoon, and working from outside to inside on both sides, are the fish fork and fish knife, followed by the meat fork and knife. Next to the dinner plate are the salad fork and knife, unless the salad is served first, in which case, it is farthest away from the plate. (See illustration on next page.)

- The simple rule about cutlery use: Always start from the outside and work your way in, course by course, toward the center.

Glasses

- Glasses follow the same progression as the silverware, moving from right to left, from the outside to the center.
- The sherry glass is positioned above the soup spoon (sherry being served to accompany soup); the white wine glass (smaller bowl than the red wine glass) is above the fish knife and the red wine glass (often served with meat) is located above the meat knife. Behind the red wine glass is the water goblet, the largest glass. The champagne flute (to accompany dessert) is to the right of the water goblet. If only a water glass is placed on the table, it would be at the tip of the knife. (See next page.)

- If the wine is cold, hold the glass by the stem. Sip from the glass and never wave it. If you are drinking red wine, it is acceptable to hold the glass by the bowl and stem, since the heat from your hand will not affect the taste of the wine. Left-handed people should remember to use the right hand to drink wine or water so it can be replaced correctly on the right hand side.
- The sherry glass is removed from the place setting when the soup plates are cleared. All the other glasses—the water goblet and the red and white wine glasses—remain on the table. You may ask to have your wine glasses removed if you will not be drinking wine.

The First Course

- The oyster fork is used to eat clams, oysters and shrimp cocktail. Because shrimp cocktail is frequently served in a pedestal dish, it would be difficult to cut the shrimp with a knife without toppling the dish. Just eat it from the fork by taking several small bites. If shrimp is served on a flat plate, you may use your knife to cut it. The lettuce in the dish is not to be eaten. It is for decoration only.
- The wait staff will remove this course from the right then place your soup plate and saucer from the left.

The Soup Course

- You will find your soup spoon on the right. Lean forward slightly to eat your soup, dip the spoon sideways into the soup at the edge nearest you. Just skim the surface of the soup and move the spoon away from you.
- Sip silently from the side of the spoon without making any noise. Don't put the entire spoon in your mouth. If you must have that last little bit, tip the bowl away from you and continue to spoon the soup from the outer edge of the bowl.
- If the soup is served in a cup with handles on both sides, it is perfectly appropriate to pick up the cup by both handles and sip the soup. Remember I am talking about a clear broth soup. Don't tip and pick up a bowl of tortilla soup just because it has handles.
- If you are served crackers with your soup course, put the soup spoon down and take a bite of the cracker. (Remember, if soup is served in a cup, the spoon rests on the plate beneath, but if soup is served in a larger bowl,

the spoon stays in the bowl.) Do not hold the cracker in one hand, the soup spoon in the other, and alternate between them. Don't break crackers into your soup. Use the same procedure as for bread. Break off the bite that you will eat and then place the remaining cracker on the under plate. If oyster crackers are served, place them on your under plate and add a few at a time to your soup.

Bread and Butter

- Usually there are bread and butter plates at a formal dinner but this is one practice that may be evolving. If there are no bread plates, do not ask for them.
- In meals, the bread and butter plate will be to your left. A separate butter knife may be resting on the plate. If there is no butter knife, it is appropriate to use your dinner knife to butter your bread or roll. Leave the knife on the bread plate until the main course is served; then move it to the entrée plate.

- In very casual settings you may find only a bread basket on the table with a shared butter dish. Offer the basket to your guests before serving yourself. (Pass to the right.) Use your clean fork to place a pat of butter on your dinner plate and put your bread or roll on the plate.
- Remember the rule to always break bread, never cut it. Then butter only a small piece that you will eat at that time. Do the same with rolls. It is inappropriate to sit at the table with half a buttered roll in your hand, taking bites as you are talking to other people at the table.
- Don't forget my little trick about the "b" and "d" and BMW from Chapter Six.

The Fish Course

- For a fish course, you will probably have a fish knife. It has a distinctive, sword-like shape.
- Hold the fish knife like a pencil so you can use the broad side of the blade to lift and separate sections of the fish.
- If you are served a boneless fillet, you will not need to use the fish knife. Leave it on the table and cut the fillet with the side of the fish fork. This fork is on your extreme left and resembles a salad fork except the tines are wider. If you would like, you can use your knife to push the food if you are eating in the Continental or European style.

The Salad

- Salads can be served before the entrée or after it, immediately before dessert. The cutlery will be placed according to the timing of this course. You may use your

66

knife to cut a lettuce leaf to bite size.

- If not set in front of you as a separate course, the salad plate will be on your left, above/beside the bread and butter plate. If entrée and salad are served at the same time, you may use the entrée fork for both.
- When the main courses are finished, the waiter will clear the table, removing the salt and pepper shakers and sweeping away crumbs. The glasses will remain. Remember not to stack your plates or to hand your plate(s) to the wait staff. Allow them to handle the removal.

Dessert

- In formal dining, the waiter will bring the dessert plate, upon which will be the finger bowl on its doily, with the dessert fork and spoon.
- Place the silverware on the table on either side of the plate. Lightly dip your fingertips into the bowl and pat gently on the towel provided or on your napkin. Then move the bowl and doily to the upper left of your plate.
- If using European or Continental style, you can eat with the spoon and use the fork as the pusher. If eating American style, you may use whichever piece of silverware you prefer and leave the other on the table. Or you may also use the other piece of silverware as a pusher.
- If fruits are served, they are quartered first with a sharp fruit knife and then peeled. Move discarded peel and any seeds to the side of your plate. Then cut the fruit into bite-sized pieces, which you eat with the fruit fork or, in an informal setting, with your fingers.
- Remember in business settings if your guest or customer does not want coffee or dessert, then your meal is over.

Don't make them sit there watching you indulge in the yummy cheesecake or leisurely drinking a cappuccino. By refusing dessert, they could be telling you the meeting is over, they need to get back to their office or they are on a diet and do not want to be tempted. You could affect the entire outcome of the meeting because you have a sweet tooth.

Finger Bowls

- Just dip the tips of your fingers into the finger bowl. Dry them on the napkin or a towel if provided. You may touch the tips of your moistened fingers to your lips and then lightly touch your napkin to your lips.
- At a dinner party in someone's home, a small crystal bowl of cool water might be presented at the beginning of the dessert course. In this case, the finger bowl is placed on a small lace or organdy doily that rests on a dessert plate. After using the finger bowl, move it with the doily to the upper left of the place setting, near where the butter plate was or just above where the forks originally were. Your empty dessert plate is now ready for the dessert.
- If you get totally confused, just watch your host or hostess. Hopefully they know what to do. But if they pick up the finger bowl and start to drink, you might not want to follow that lead.

Inedible Items

- The simple rule is to take inedible items out of your mouth the same way they were put in. In other words, remove grape seeds with your fingers, because you eat grapes with your fingers; gristle is removed with your fork; pits, such as prune pits, are removed with a spoon. But, I do disagree on this etiquette rule. If you have been trying diligently to eat apiece of meat unsuccessfully, I strongly suggest you bring your napkin discreetly to your mouth and place the meat in the napkin. You do not need to spit it into the napkin. Then ask the wait staff to replace your napkin.

- The only exception is a fish bone. Although fish is eaten with a fork, you remove a fish bone from your mouth with your fingers. Place whatever you are removing at the edge of your plate.

Salt and Pepper

- The salt and pepper always travel together, even if someone requests only one. Place the shakers on the table in front of the person requesting them. Do not hand them to the person. Just remember that they "are married."
- You may encounter a little dish of salt called a salt cellar. Pass the salt cellar with the pepper shaker. The salt cellar usually has an accompanying tiny salt spoon. Use it to place a spoonful of salt at the edge of your plate and dip each forkful of food into that. If there is no spoon, use the edge of your clean knife to serve yourself a portion of salt.

Wine Selection

- Wines are changing, and the steadfast principle of white wine with fish and poultry and red wine with meat is not necessarily the rule of thumb.Now it is more your choice and your taste. This little guideline may help you remember:

- *CHardonnay* and *CHablis* go well with CHicken.
- *SOave* is good with SOle.
- *BEaujolais* is a red wine to drink with BEef, as are *B*ordeaux and *B*arolo.

- Usually wines served during a meal are described as "dry," which means that they are not sweet. However, champagne is labeled differently. A champagne marked dry, or sec, is the sweetest of sparkling wines. Extra dry will be a bit less sweet. The driest champagnes are labeled brut.
- The sommelier will be happy to advise you. By all means, rely upon the wine steward's expertise and allow him to assist you in choosing appropriate wines.
- Here are some simple estimates for wine servings:
  - Three bottles of wine for a table of eight
  - Five servings per 750 ml (normal size) bottle of wine
  - Ten servings per magnum (1.5 liters) of wine

Serving Beer

Before beer was for picnics, night clubs and sitting around eating pizza, but now it is much more acceptable even in nicer, upscale restaurants. Be prepared when guests ask for beer instead of wine.

- Have nice, attractive pilsner glasses or even fun steins (with no advertisements on them) for serving beer.

Oversized red wine goblets also are acceptable. Stay away from the tumblers or plastic glasses you use for water or soda.

- Do not put cans or bottles of beer on the table. Pour the beer into a tall glass that will hold the entire contents of the bottle or can.
- Beer usually is served with hearty, simple food. Beer goes well with sandwiches, hamburgers, pizza, Tex-Mex food, oriental food, picnics and barbecues. Avoid ordering beer in a fine restaurant with a delicate fish or a rich gourmet dessert.
- If you are dining with an executive who orders wine or a cocktail with the meal, it is fine for you to order beer.
- Do not walk around a reception or cocktail party carrying a bottle or can of beer. Have it poured into a nice, tall glass.
- You may serve beer instead of wine at a business luncheon, but make sure the menu is informal and proper glasses are available. Always offer guests alternatives such as wine, iced tea or coffee.

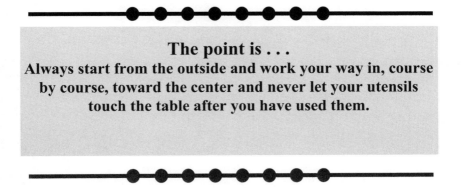

The point is . . .

Always start from the outside and work your way in, course by course, toward the center and never let your utensils touch the table after you have used them.

EIGHT

Hosting and Attending Business Meals

Hosting a well-planned business meal presents many challenges but can leave a lasting good impression on your clients. Remember when you are participating in a business meal as either host or guest you represent your company and your behavior reflects on your employer as well as yourself. Although the dining table may seem more informal than the conference table, you must always demonstrate the highest professionalism and courtesy.

Seated Dinners

- If you are hosting, arrive early to finalize all plans. This includes the flow of the meal, seating arrangements, name badges, handling the bill in advance and meeting wait staff.
- If you do not have a private room or area in the restaurant, then make sure you select an area that is a little more secluded or away from the kitchen and the main part of the facility.
- Make sure as your guests arrive that you or a staff person meets them at the door to direct them to your seating area or reception. If it is a smaller dinner, then greet your guests at the table and introduce yourself, if necessary. Shake hands. If name badges are required, guests should receive them immediately.
- As host, you should control the luncheon/dinner. If you want specific seating, arrive early so you can place guests as they enter. If possible, use place cards for guests and

place them according to rank if appropriate. (See "Table Seating" in this chapter.)

- As host, try to keep your back to the wall in order to see everyone who is coming toward you. Be sure to arrange to have good eye contact between yourself and the most important client.

- If you are a guest, wait to sit down until you receive your host's signal. If your host sits down without signaling you where to sit, take the chair nearest you. When the waiter seats you, take the chair he offers. It usually is the best at that table.

- Enter from your left when you sit at a table and leave from the right.

- If you are introducing co-workers or clients, be specific about their names and titles and possibly even the roles they will play in the particular event, function or project you're discussing.

- Remember, no purses or other items should be placed on the table. If you have a briefcase or purse, put it to the right of your chair or underneath your chair. You should leave from the right of the chair and can pick it up easily and quickly. Be careful not to trip on the straps of a purse or briefcase and be sure to place them out of the way of wait staff.

- Wait until the entire table is served before eating. If a person's meal is delayed for some reason and he instructs you to start eating, go ahead. If there is a host, follow his cue. If you are the host, make a nice comment for guests to start and to enjoy their meals. Even if all have been served, wait until the host or the guest of honor starts to eat.

- If you are seated at a long table with more than the standard eight to ten people, then wait for at least four to six people in that particular area to be served before starting to eat. In large table settings it is too difficult to make sure all 16 or 20 have been served. But if you know a toast or prayer is to be given before the start of the meal, then all must wait until all are served and the necessary comments are made.

- Place your napkin on the chair if you need to leave the table, and push your chair in. (Remember my comment in Chapter Six that placing your napkin on the chair bothers some people.) When you return, the waiter may have refolded your napkin and placed it on the back or the arm of the chair. Remember not to refold the napkin at the end of the meal. Just pick it up from the center and place it loosely on the table to the left of the plate.
- If time permits, order your meal before you start business. The best situation is to wait for business until after the meal while you are having coffee/drinks, but time constraints and the situation will prevail.
- Don't spread out your papers over the table. This is not your desk or work area.
- A man should unbutton his jacket at the table but when he stands, button it again.
- Don't sit back and cross your arms during a business meal. Or even worse, rock your chair on the back two legs.
- Wine may be offered with your meal. If you choose not to have wine with your meal, just tell the wait staff you will not be having any wine or place your fingertips lightly on the rim of the glass when the server approaches. Never turn your glass upside down. Just say, "I will not be having wine today/tonight." To release the bouquet of red wine and brandy, hold the glasses by the bowl so the warmth of your hand will enhance the taste. Red wine glasses may be held by the stem, but white wine and champagne glasses

are always held by the stem to keep the chill of the glass.

- Never lift your glassware or cup when someone is pouring. Just let it sit on the table and the wait staff will come to it.
- Always remember to take your cue from the hosts. Once they have lifted their glasses, you may follow.
- See Chapter Six "Dining and Table Etiquette" for more helpful hints.

Visual Signs for the Wait Staff

- Imagine a clock on your plate. To indicate you are finished eating, place both the knife and fork in about the 10:20 position of a clock with the points at 10 and the handles at 20 after, or the 4. The tines of the fork can be up or down, and the blade of the knife should be facing you. If eating American style, the fork tines are up and if eating  Continental style, the tines are down. If you have been eating the course with the fork only, place it tines up in the 10:20 position when finished.
- Another easy sign for the wait staff is to just place the fork and knife side by side on the right-hand rim of the plate. The fork is inside the knife and with the fork tines up or down. The blade of the knife should be turned inward.

- If resting while eating in the Continental/European style, place the knife and fork in an inverted V formation. The blade of the knife should be toward the center of the plate, with the tip of the knife aimed at 12 and the bottom at 4. The tines of the fork should point down and be aimed at 12, with the bottom of the handle at 8.

- The other resting position for eating American style is to place the knife across the top of the plate horizontally with the blade facing toward you and the fork placed diagonally across the plate as similar to the finished position at 10:20 with the tines up.

Table Seating

Many considerations are involved in proper seating, including rank, foreign dignitaries and guests, religious, elderly, military and executives. The No. 1 principle of seating by rank is to seat the most important person on the host's right and the next most important on the host's left and then to seat the third and fourth most important people on the co-host's right and left.

Executive Host

Guest #1		Guest #2
Guest #5		Guest #6
Guest #4		Guest #3

Co-host

Making Introductions and "HOW"

- Always stand for introductions and to shake hands. If you can't stand up completely because you are seated at a table or just wedged in a back area, at least stand partially from the chair to show respect. I am sure the other person will tell you to sit back down for your own comfort. Just remember to always try to stand to put yourself on the same level as the person who is approaching you to shake hands and a start a conversation.
- Scenario: At a reception, you are standing, talking to a group of people. A person walks up to talk to you and you want to introduce him or her to the group but are unsure of someone's name in the group. You should introduce the new person and then ask everyone in the group to introduce themselves. It avoids embarrassment for you and it allows everyone in the group to be a little more involved.
- Always include a little explanation with your introductions. This could include telling a little about their position at their company, the time they have been involved with the company or project or something that could keep the conversation going and add a little information for the new people to become instantly involved in the conversation. This works extremely well if you introduce two new

people and then leave them. They will have at least a little chit-chat to continue the conversation and hopefully move into more business conversations.

- Scenario: You approach a table at which there are people already seated. Move around the table, introducing yourself to everyone before you sit down. It is better than sitting there for an hour or more with no idea who is seated across from you. You are missing great connecting opportunities.

- The "HOW" is a technique that sets the groundwork for introductions. The "H" standing for higher ranking person, the "O" is for older and the "W" is for woman. This is a general guideline but, of course, there will be times when this rule could overlap. The number one rule to remember is rank. The higher ranking or more important person's name is said first. "Senator Lott, this is Rick Wayne, the precinct chairman." In the past, gender was very important but introductions today need to concentrate on the higher ranking and not the gender. But there are times when an older person or a woman should be respected and introduced first.

    o A young person is introduced to an older person. "Dr. Lauren, I'd like you to meet my nephew, Hudson Campbell." "Tammy, this is my dear friend, Olivia."

    o A man introduced to a woman. "Mrs. Smith, I'd like you to meet Mr. Albert." The exception is if the man is a head of state, royalty, a church official or an older man in a high position.

- Not introducing a person is the worst social mistake you can make. Introduce a visitor who comes into your office, a new employee to members of the staff, a client to your boss or even a friend at a party. Introductions are more relaxed than they were in the past, but not introducing people as they enter a room or a meeting is not acceptable.

- If you have a sudden mental block and forget names when making introductions, just make a sincere apology with a big smile. It happens to everyone, so they will forgive you and hopefully tell you their names.
- If you see someone is struggling to introduce you, state your name yourself and offer a handshake.
- If a married woman does not use her husband's name, make sure the names and relationships are clear in the beginning without belaboring the issue.
- See Chapter Five for more details on introductions.

Making a Toast

- Never toast yourself. If a person offers a toast to you then stay seated, respond with a thank-you and do not take a drink or hold the glass. If you are standing as part of a reception and you have a drink in your hand, then just stand there, do not motion with the glass and again just say, "Thank you."
- Be brief and speak from your heart when you offer a toast. Thirty to sixty seconds is more than enough. Never have a note card to read the toast. If you can't remember it or memorize it, then it is too long.
- You may return a toast immediately or later near the end of the meal.
- Do not tap or click your glass to get everyone's attention. Just stand and ask for everyone's attention and the room should start to quiet. If there is a band, you can request a change in the tone of music to signal for attention or move to the microphone to ask for their attention.

- It is not necessary that everyone clang or tap their glasses together to signify the toast. You can motion with the glass or nod to each person and then take a drink. It is an old tradition and hard to break.
- A toast can be made with whatever you may be drinking. It does not need to be an alcoholic drink.
- You may make a toast to more than one person. It can be to congratulate or thank an entire department, division or team.
- When you raise your glass for a toast, do not take it higher than your eyes or shoulder height.
- The host should always be the first one to make a toast.
- If you are entertaining international clients or guests and want to toast them in their native language, be sure to learn the correct pronunciation beforehand. Otherwise, stick to your native tongue. There are many variations in toasting rituals, so try and understand and respect other cultures and traditions.

Buffets

- After everyone is seated and drink orders are taken, the host should gesture for everyone to go to the buffet. If there is no host, a more senior person should make the signal to begin.
- Serve yourself reasonable portions. You can go back for more.
- If an item appears to be in short in supply, be conservative. At a restaurant, you can ask the wait staff to replenish, but at a private home, never inquire about more. Usually in a private home, all the food will be displayed at one time.

- Place the serving spoon or fork next to the platter or chafing dish. Do not leave it in the serving dish.
- Don't bring back enough food or desserts for everyone at your table. Bring enough for your own meal unless someone at your table needs assistance or specifically asks you to bring back an item.
- At serving stations, limit your requests. Be considerate of the people in line behind you. If you must have a special item, wait until the main rush has already gone through the lines.
- Replace your plate each time you return to a buffet. Never reuse the same plate.
- Don't scrape or stack your plates on the table.
- Be courteous to the people around you. Even though people leave and return to the table, be polite when eating. If you are the first one back to the table, it is polite to wait for at least one other person to join you before you start to eat.
- If there are at least three people seated at your table for a buffet, always avoid leaving one person seated at the table while two of you run off to replenish your plates. You should take turns so that two are seated at the table eating and visiting while the third person goes to replenish their dish. It is difficult to get the timing just right but always try to avoid sitting by yourself and eating or leaving a lone person at the table.
- If you want desert and know the others at your table do not, then bring the desert back with your entree to avoid leaving the table again.

Receptions

- It's difficult to conduct business and meet someone new when you are constantly eating or drinking and your hands are full. If you must have a drink or eat some food then do it one at a time so your right hand is always free.
- No matter how you try it is still awkward. Try not to come to a reception when you are absolutely famished. Work the room and then ask a prospective customer to join you for a drink or some food.
- Focus on the opportunity to meet people and work the room. Wear your name badge, if appropriate, and make it very visible for people to read.
- Have ample business cards ready to hand out. Again, that is difficult if your hands are full with food and drink.
- See Chapter Four "Connecting and Getting the Best End Results."

Additional Business Meal Tips

- Mingle. Get to know other guests and your hosts at a function or event.
- When attending a hosted event for your company, spend the time visiting with the company staff that is hosting you. Do not visit for any length of time with co-workers you see daily.
- If your company hosts an employee event, sit with other departments and introduce yourself to people you do not see regularly. Do not socialize only within your own department.
- If you have the opportunity to order off a menu, order

what you normally would when you are paying for the meal. Be conservative. Don't order highly priced items or specialty drinks. Never ask to take your food home when you are attending a business meal. Doggie bags are a big "no-no."

- Follow the lead of your hosts. If they order smaller meals, you don't have to have just a cup of soup but don't order a four-course meal either. Also, if they pass on dessert and coffee, you should too. Possibly that is a sign they need to return to the office and there is not enough time for another course.

- Hosting business meals can be challenging for a woman, especially if the guests are men. The female host should be sure to arrange for payment in advance with the restaurant manager so there will be no issue of who picks up the tab.

- For businesswomen traveling and dining alone, I recommend taking a seat against the wall to be able to see others approaching.

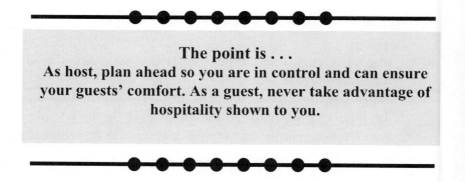

The point is . . .
As host, plan ahead so you are in control and can ensure your guests' comfort. As a guest, never take advantage of hospitality shown to you.

NINE

Handling Difficult Foods

The best way to deal with difficult foods is to avoid ordering them, but occasionally you have no choice. Some foods are challenging to deal with gracefully. Here is a short alphabetical list of some problem foods and tips for handling them. Remember, at times it is perfectly correct to eat some foods with your fingers. The general rule is, when in doubt, use cutlery correctly. If you have already touched an item, go ahead and eat it with your fingers.

Apples and Pears
At a formal dinner, when the fruit knife and fork are presented, quarter and peel the fruit, if you wish, then slice into bite-sized pieces and eat with a fork.

Apricots
At a formal dinner, halve the apricot, cut out the pit and eat with a fork.

Artichokes
Artichokes may be served hot or cold. Tear off one leaf at a time, dip the broad end into the accompanying melted butter or Hollandaise sauce, then bring it to your mouth and gently draw the meat out by running the leaf between your teeth. Place the leaves neatly on your plate (if a separate bowl is not provided). You will come to the fuzzy choke, which is inedible. Remove it with your knife and fork to reveal the saucer-shaped artichoke heart, which should be eaten with a knife and fork. Because you have used your fingers to eat the leaves, you should be served a

finger bowl when you are finished. During a business meal, this time-consuming and intense ritual draws your attention away from the client, who should be your prime concern, so artichokes would not be an appropriate choice.

Asparagus

These are finger foods. It is okay to pick up a stalk at the base, dip the tip into the accompanying sauce and bite off the head. Many people are unaware of this, however, so if your client uses knife and fork to cut asparagus, by all means do the same. Individual tongs are sometimes brought in with asparagus and they may be used instead of your fingers to grasp the base. When asparagus is overcooked and soft, it is best to use your knife and fork. Any part of the base that is too tough to chew is left on the side of the plate.

Avocado

If it is served cut in half with the pit removed, eat it with a spoon. If peeled, cut up and served with a salad, it is eaten with a fork.

Bacon

The correct way to eat bacon is with a fork. If it is extremely crisp and dry, the fingers may be used.

Bananas

In a formal setting, the banana should be peeled, cut into slices and eaten with a fork.

Berries

In a formal setting, berries are eaten with a spoon. A large berry, such as a strawberry, may be eaten with a fruit fork and knife. If the berries are served whole with the hull attached, you may hold each at the hull and dip the berry into the accompanying sauce, cream or sugar. To eat a giant chocolate-dipped strawberry, insert the fork into the flesh near the stem and slice the berry vertically several times and cut off the stem. Do this carefully so you don't destroy the chocolate coating.

Bread
When you are served an uncut loaf of bread, you may cut or break off your own slice then pass the loaf to the person to your right. The host may decide to cut the entire loaf and then pass the cut bread to the others at the table. An excellent alternative is to ask your server to take it back to the kitchen to have it cut. It is a nice solution and avoids everyone at the table touching the bread. When you are breaking your bread and crumbs fall all over the table, you can very nonchalantly pick up a few crumbs and place them on the plate. No one will notice. Just don't make one big sweeping motion and brush them to the floor. You can always just wait and the server will either brush them into a clean napkin or remove them with a clever little metal container called a "crumber." This process generally happens between the entrée and your dessert.

Butter
Use the clean dinner fork to bring the butter to your plate; use the butter knife to spread butter on bread (one bite at a time). Butter is put on a baked potato with your fork, not your knife.

Canapes
Served before a meal, they are finger foods; served at the table, they are eaten with a fork.

Caviar
Spread caviar on toast with a knife, hold the toast with your fingers and take one bite at a time.

Celery, Radishes and Pickles
Take relishes off the service plate with your fingers, place them on your dinner plate and eat them with your fingers. If there are tongs on the service plate, use them to move these relishes to your plate.

Cherries or Other Fruits with Pits
If these fruits are eaten with the fingers in an informal setting, remove the pit from your mouth into your hand and place the pit on the edge of your plate. At a formal setting, when served in a dessert, a spoon is used. Bring the spoon to your mouth and put the pit into the spoon and place it on the edge of your plate.

Chicken or Fowl
Unless you are at a picnic or barbecue, chicken is not a finger food. Use your knife and fork.

Chops (of any kind)
The chicken rule applies. Although the tastiest meat may be closest to the bone, if you can't cut it off with your knife and fork, the meat must remain on your plate.

Clams
Whether they are baked or served on the half shell, clams are eaten in one bite. Use the oyster fork to pick up the clam. You may then pick up the shell and drink the remaining clam juice. For steamed clams, open the shell and with your fingers pull away the black outer skin covering the neck. Holding the neck, dip the clam into the accompanying broth or melted butter and eat it in one mouthful. This complicated, time-consuming and potentially messy ritual makes steamers inadvisable at a business meal.

Corn on the Cob

Corn on the cob is served only in a very informal setting. Hold it with both hands and butter just a few rows at a time. This food is never served on formal occasions. In Europe, corn on the cob is considered food for livestock.

Crackers

Be cautious with crackers. Do not break them into soup and do not hold a cracker in one hand and the soup spoon in the other. Treat crackers like bread.

Éclair

It's best to eat all pastries with a fork.

Eggs

To eat a boiled egg in a cup, crack the shell gently with a knife, lift off the shell, and place it on the edge of the plate. Steady the egg cup with one hand and eat the egg with the other hand, using a spoon.

Escargots (Snails)

Escargots are usually served with a special pair of tongs and a double-pronged fork. Grip the snail shell in the tongs, and pull out the snail with the fork. If there's bread at the table, it is perfectly correct (and delicious) to dip the bread into the garlic sauce after you have eaten the snails. This is another tricky selection for business meals.

Fish

Generally a fish fillet is eaten with a fish fork. If fish is presented whole, you can ask the server to fillet it. They will either remove your plate and have it done in the kitchen or will make a small production and choreograph the process right at your table. Also if your fish comes with its head, you can ask the server to take it and remove the head. You can remove it yourself and then set it to the side of your plate. If all these bones and head are a little too much for you, then ask for a small plate to place the head and skeleton on and then have the waiter remove all of it so you can enjoy your meal. To fillet the fish yourself, place the fish knife, if provided, or your dinner knife under the backbone. Using your knife and fork, fold back the top half of the fish, exposing the bone. You can then lift the entire bone structure out and place it on the side of your plate. Then eat the fish with your fish fork. If you find a small bone in a bite, take it from your mouth with your thumb and forefinger and place it on the edge of your plate. Again, this may be too much of a procedure for a business meal.

French Fries
If fries are served with a burger, then use your fingers, but if served in a more formal setting, cut in half and use a fork.

Grapefruit Halves
Section these fruits to avoid a lot of digging with the spoon. Never squeeze the juice.

Hard-shell Crabs and Lobsters
Crack the shell with a nutcracker and use your seafood fork (a small utensil with three tines) to remove the meat. If it is a large piece of meat, cut it with a fork. Pull off the small claws and treat them as if you were drawing liquid through a straw. Stuffed lobster is eaten with a knife and fork. This is another food that you should think twice about ordering when entertaining a client.

Lemons
Cup a lemon in your hand to avoid squirting anyone as you squeeze it over tea or seafood.

Mussels

Mussels may be removed from the shell with a fork, dipped into the sauce and eaten in one bite. In a more informal setting, you may pick up the shell, scoop a little of the juice with it and suck the mussel and juice directly off the shell. Place the empty shells in a bowl or plate that should be provided.

Oysters

There are various ways to prepare and eat oysters. If on the half shell, steady the shell on the plate with one hand, and with the other hand use an oyster fork to lift out the oyster, which you then place in your mouth whole and chew, if necessary. You may pick up the shell and drink the juice after you have eaten the oyster. Oysters in a stew are eaten with a spoon. Fried oysters are eaten with a knife and fork.

Parfait

Start at the top using the long parfait spoon usually served with this dessert and inch your way down to the syrup at the bottom. Don't try to stir the syrup or fruits to the top.

Pasta

Pasta can present problems. My first suggestion is to just cut it to be safe. Otherwise, using your fork, separate a few strands and twirl the fork against a larger spoon or the edge of the plate to gather the strands onto it. Make sure the bite is not too large and unmanageable. It is difficult to avoid dripping sauce, splashing sauce or just having problems with pasta. If you have a choice, don't order it at a business meal.

Peas

This is one time you could use your bread or roll to assist you. If eating American style with just fork in your hand, then use bread, roll or even your spoon to help out. If you eat Continental or European style, it is a little easier to have your fork in your left hand and then shovel with your knife in your right hand. If it is too hard for you to maneuver, then try to get a few peas and leave the rest.

Petits Fours

These small cakes are finger foods and are eaten in small bites. If they are presented on paper wrappers, take the wrapper from the serving dish with your selection.

Potato, Baked

Cut an X in the top, squeeze the potato slightly with your fingers, and then add butter and/or sour cream. If you add butter, use your fork. Don't try to convert the inside into mashed potatoes. If you want to eat the skin, cut it into small pieces with a knife and fork.

Shrimp

If the tails are left on, then eat shrimp with your fingers. Shrimp cocktail should be eaten with a seafood fork, in two bites if large, or you can put the shrimp on a plate and cut them with a knife and fork.

Sushi and Sashimi

Eat sushi pieces whole if they are small enough or cut them with a knife and fork or with the ends of chopsticks. It is also proper to use your fingers to eat sushi.

Tomatoes, Cherry
It's difficult to chase cherry tomatoes around your plate and they usually are too large to eat whole, so it is best to use a knife and fork to cut them into pieces. Be careful because they will squirt.

Watermelon
Use a spoon when watermelon is in small balls. Otherwise, use a fork and knife. Put the seeds in the palm of your hand and then transfer them to your plate.

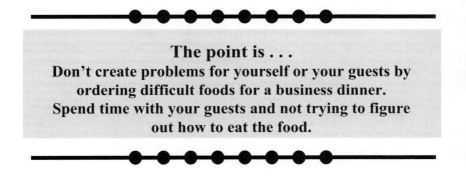

The point is . . .
Don't create problems for yourself or your guests by ordering difficult foods for a business dinner. Spend time with your guests and not trying to figure out how to eat the food.

TEN

Working in a Home Office

Is working out of your home really for you? Millions of people seem to think it works for them and thousands more are starting to work out of their homes every day. There are many reasons people are working from their homes or a satellite office. It is a great idea if you are just starting your own company. Financially, it is smart to work from your home and avoid the overhead expenses of a building or an office suite. Perhaps your company is downsizing or is running out of office space and has asked you to work from your home. Possibly you decided to quit your job and start to freelance. There are many reasons for leaving the corporate office space and finding comfort in your own home. But moving to a home or virtual office is a major transition. You need to review the advantages and disadvantages of working independently, establish a start-up budget, get organized and create routines for working from home.

Possible Disadvantages of Working from a Home Office

- No support staff, or at least not at arm's length
- Smaller storage space
- No heavy-duty copier machine handy
- No in-house postal service
- Less socializing with co-workers
- The cost of setting up your own office

- Having to be everything: the receptionist, switchboard operator, administrative assistant, mail room person, head of purchasing, chief of finance, customer service and sales and marketing staff
- More self-discipline and less guidance
- The challenge of separating your personal life from professional business during the day
- The perception of others that you are not really working

Possible Advantages of Working from a Home Office

- Independence
- Efficiency of working with fewer interruptions
- Being in control of your own schedule
- No dress code
- No office politics
- No commute time and no traffic to fight
- Low overhead costs after start-up

Finding/Making Space for a Home Office

- Many people think they will just convert a part of their dining room or use the little alcove in their bedroom for an office. Chances are this will not work. You need to evaluate your home and decide if you have the necessary space. You need room for a permanent desk, chair, computer hook up, file cabinets, separate phone lines, fax machine, printer, storage space, sufficient electrical outlets and good lighting. Plus, it's an advantage if you can work away from major distractions.

- If clients need to come to your home office for a meeting, will you have a separate entrance to your office or will they need to walk through most of your home to get to your office or meeting space? You need to decide. It might be better to meet at their office or at another convenient location.
- Do you need to create a completely new area by constructing a new space, converting an existing area or remodeling a particular room, basement or even a larger closet? It is amazing what you can do with existing areas. The costs and the time of building or remodeling must be factored into your plans for a starting date as well as your budget.
- A consultation with a professional office organizer may save you time, money and energy in the long run.

Getting Organized in Your New Office

When you find the best space in your home, you must get organized. Your new office at home may have less space than your corporate office. Even if you are fortunate and have a large area, the space must be designed properly. Take your time in the beginning and work out a floor plan that fits your space, needs and budget. But, you say, you must get moved into your new office immediately and start working. Believe me, the time you invest initially will save you time in the long run. Begin with a good plan. After you have found the right space for your office, you must:

- Set up the office so it is functional.
- Have a plan. It may take a while to create this plan, but think through the process and make sure you select

what fits your needs and office space.

- Consider the costs involved. Do you have most of your equipment and furniture, or do you need to buy it? If so, then consider your budget. If your budget is limited, then buy the office equipment first and save the furniture for later. But make sure you consider private phone lines, a good office phone, computer/ printers and fax machine. Do not buy office equipment knowing that within a year you will need to upgrade. Possibly your corporate office will provide equipment for you or you can purchase equipment at reduced rates. But just remember the desk that worked in your nice, big corporate office may overwhelm your new home office.

- Use a grid to chart out the space for your furnishings. Measure exactly how much space you have and then chart it on the grid. Don't buy equipment and furniture and hope it fits in your office. The grid or floor plan will allow you to move around templates of a desk, chair and file cabinets so you can see the actual setup.

- Organize and find a place for your files and office supplies. Get rid of old files and unnecessary items. Don't just move them around. If you don't need them, throw them away. If you just move them to another area, you will have the same problem later.   Put them on your computer.

- Think for efficiency and organization. If you think and operate professionally, you will work professionally.

- If your second office is your car, organize so you can operate efficiently. Keep a container to hold files that can easily be accessed for your next meeting. Don't attempt to talk on a cell phone, send out an e-mail or work as you drive.

Estimating Equipment and Initial Set-up Costs

Costs for setting up your office will vary tremendously. You may be starting with absolutely nothing or may already own some equipment and need to buy some items. Decide what is critical to begin your office and how much you can afford to spend. Buy only the absolute essentials in the beginning and then add items as you need them or can afford them. Always look for sales at office supply stores and computer stores. Below is a very basic list of what you may need and the range of costs to purchase these items.

Bookshelves	$50-$200
Chair(s)	$75-$200 +
Computer (desktop)	$1000-$2000
Computer desk	$125-$500
Credenza/Work table	$100-$300 +
Desk	$150-$400 +
Fax machine	$200-$600
File cabinets	$100-$500
Floor mat	$25-$125
ISDN lines	$150/line (varies by location)
Lamps	$15-$200
Laptop	$1000-$3000 (watch for specials)
Phone lines (2-3)	$150-$250 (plus answering service)
Phone(s)	Monthly charges (plus initial installation)
Printer (color/B&W)	$100-$300
Scanner	$75-$400
Stationery/Business cards	$50-$1500
Web site construction	$500-$2000 +

Of course, costs can vary widely depending on your needs and your tastes. You may already have or want to purchase other items for your office including additional furniture, a clock, radio, waste paper baskets, calculator, electric three-hole punch, personal digital assistant (Various electronic devices are now available and costs depend on your needs, wants and budget.) postage scale and meter, electric pencil sharpener or electric stapler.

Purchasing Office Supplies

Working from home takes away the advantage of walking into the corporate office supply room and taking what you need. Now you must evaluate your initial needs and buy items that will need to be replenished as well as items that you will need to purchase only once. Some of the supplies include:

Binders and tab dividers	Mailing envelopes
CDs/DVDs	Manila folders
Cover stock paper	Message stamps
Dictionary/Thesaurus	Note pads
Expense reports	Paper (copy, computer, fax)
File folders	Paper clips
Hanging folders with tabs	Pens/Pencils
Highlighters and markers	Rubber bands
Hole puncher(s)	Scissors
Ink cartridges	Stapler, staples
Invoices/Petty cash book	Stapler remover
Labels (folders, mailing)	Stamps
Laser printer paper	Sticky notes
Legal Pads	Tape and dispenser

Your specific type of work and office space will determine the supplies you need. Keep supplies as well stocked as possible. Watch for sales at office supply stores but don't buy something just because it is on sale. Keep a list handy to check off when you need supplies and take it with you when you go to the office supply store. It is more efficient to work from a list. Remember your storage space and try to buy only what you need.

What Belongs on Your Desk?

The answer is: as little as possible. Some people insist on a clean desk and some just love to work in clutter. It's hard to change either person, but clutter can and will interfere with your productivity. Here are some desktop guidelines:

- The computer is the centerpiece of the desk. Position it first.
- Your printer can be on or next to your desk.
- Put the fax machine on an extended desktop or close to your desk.
- You may need a lamp on your desk in addition to overhead lights or if you have no overhead lights.
- Keep on your desk only items that you use daily.
- Keep close at hand items that you use weekly.
- Keep pens, tablets, stapler, stapler remover, tape, etc., organized and ready to use but, preferably, in a drawer.
- Organize items to work to your advantage. If you are right-handed, put your phone on the left side so you can take notes, or vice versa for left-handers. Headsets for phones are also great tools.

What Belongs in Desk Drawers and File Cabinets?

The first thing you need to do is get organized. Are there stacks and stacks of papers on your desk, the floor and every possible space in your office? Do you throw them away or file them? Do you need additional file cabinets, maybe some shelves or stacking bins? Do you have space for them? Or do you need an assistant to come in periodically to organize your things?

Start with what you have. Go through your drawers one at a time and you'll be amazed at what you can get rid of quickly. Do you really need that old file? Probably not. Do you really need those old magazines or articles? Probably not. Keep what you need and throw away the rest. Scan or put material on discs.

- If you haven't used an item in a year, it is pretty safe to throw it away.
- Toss out things that don't work anymore, like old pens and highlighters.
- Use desk trays to organize drawers and maximize the space you have. Put paper clips in one section of the organizer so they are in one area and easy for you to reach and use instantly. Don't mix clips with staples and rubber bands.
- Use files to hold your paper, stationery, fax cover sheets, etc. This keeps them neat and convenient.
- Remember, with everything stored on your computer, many paper files can be eliminated.

You will save so much time by being organized and not looking for a certain sheet of stationery or a paper clip. Unfortunately, those stacks of paper seem to continue growing, so staying organized can be a continuing challenge.

Balancing Professional and Personal Life

When you work in a corporate office, it is much easier to separate yourself and start your personal life when you walk out the door. But when your office is in your home, it can become difficult to separate your personal life from your work. You need to set guidelines and be disciplined enough to keep the two as separate as possible.

- The first step is to move your office away from the busy part of your home where there is traffic and noise.
- If you have children at home with a sitter/nanny, rules about their care away from your office must be set and adhered to.
- Keep the house duties on hold until after your work hours or limit yourself to quick, simple chores like tossing a load of clothes in the washer or dryer.
- Remember, you can't be shopping or playing golf all day and achieve your business goals.

At times it can be almost impossible to keep the professional and personal completely separated but you must focus on work during business hours.

Daily Routine for a Home Office

When you worked in the corporate world, you would wake up at the same time each morning and go through your usual rituals to get ready for work. Then you would either drive or ride the bus or rail to get to your office. With an office at home, you can wake up and go directly to work. But there are disadvantages to being a few steps down the hallway from your office. You should develop a pattern similar to what you had before, just minus leaving your house.

- Schedule a regular wake-up time.
- Set routine office hours.
- Take your shower and do your normal morning rituals so in case someone calls for a last-minute appointment, you will be ready.
- Schedule a lunch time, whether you are going out or staying home.
- Try to schedule your appointments not to coincide with heavy traffic in the morning or evening.
- Try to schedule appointments on the same day or back to back so you are not making excessive trips to and from your office.
- Don't forget to do regular back-ups of your computer and personal data devices.
- Stay focused on your work but leave time to take a break.
- Don't eat breakfast or lunch at your desk.
- Schedule one full day a week to stay in your office and get things done. Try to pick the day of the week when calls are a little slower and fewer appointments are usually booked. If such a day doesn't exist, at least let your voice mail answer your calls for half a day

while you get caught up.

- Be disciplined about your routine. For some, it is too easy to work all hours of the day and night because work is close at hand. For others, it may be easy to go play that game of golf during the day and then plan to get caught up with work at night. Just remember the hours needed to contact clients or to schedule your meetings.
- Take off one day a month and enjoy it out of your office.
- Make sure your have two phone lines into your home/office. Let your personal phone line go into the answering machine.
- Learn to say no. Some of us have a problem saying no and we just keep accepting more projects, joining more committees and signing up to do more programs. We think it might help our future when, in fact, it could hurt. Taking on too much jeopardizes the quality of your work. Choose extra projects selectively. Make sure they will work for you and your career.

Postal Service

You may want to secure a special postal service account with a service company. There are many available and for a monthly fee you can get a post office box or suite number. Although having to go to this location daily or every other day is a disadvantage, there are many advantages:

- Your professional mail is delivered separately from your personal mail.
- Business contacts will not know your home address.

- A suite address gives your company a professional image.
- The postal service will accept packages and sign for them.
- You may get access to faster and larger fax and copy machines.
- Services such as overnight shipping may be available.

Receipts/Income Tax

It is critical to start a file drawer solely for your receipts. For almost a year, I was throwing all my receipts into one box. I thought that was pretty organized because they were all in one place. But, still at the end of the year, I needed to sort them to prepare my income tax. Now I do my income tax quarterly and that is so much better for my organization.

- Use separate credit cards for business and personal expenditures. It is easier to keep the two separated for tax purposes and reporting business expenses.
- Keep track of all your expenses and receipts.
- Start a file system and automatically file your receipts to keep accurate records so you will know how much money you are spending throughout the year.
- Purchase a software program such as QuickBooks so your accounting system looks professional and the checks are typed and recorded.
- When you travel, carry an expense report that can easily be transferred into your financial system and an envelope to hold all of your receipts.
- At the bottom of each receipt make sure to write the purpose of the expense and, if a client was involved, include the

name, company and purpose of the meeting/meal.

- Keep a form in your car to record mileage at the beginning and end of your business trips. Don't rely on your memory.
- If finance is not your strongest asset, you may need to hire a CPA/bookkeeper to assist you with setting up your finances, handling your income tax withdrawals and reporting your income tax. It may cost a little more but in the long run, it will be beneficial. You'll save time and frustration and have support if you are audited.

Suggested Files for a Financial System

Advertising/Promotion
Bank loans
Bank statements
Car/Mileage/Tolls/Parking
Charge accounts
Educational materials
Educational seminars/
  Conventions
Gifts
Hotel expenses
Insurance
Investments
  (pension, profit-sharing, SEP)
Invoices
Legal costs

Marketing
Meals and entertainment
Memberships/Dues
Office equipment
Office supplies
Postage (including box rentals)
Printing
Rent
Salaries/Contract labor
Stationery/Business cards
Tax deductions/Charities
Telephone (office and cell)
Travel (airfare, car rental,
  ground transportation)
Utilities

Staying in Touch with the Corporate World

It is important to be involved with professional organizations and to stay in contact with your peers. Some people fear if they work from home, others will forget about them and their value in the job market will be diminished. If anything, it has been proven that people who work from their homes are more productive and reach their goals and quotas. If you conduct all your business at the highest professional level, many of your clients and contacts will never be aware that you work from a home office.

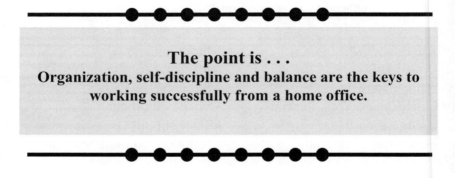

The point is . . .
Organization, self-discipline and balance are the keys to working successfully from a home office.

ELEVEN

Packing for Business Travel

After traveling for business for at least three decades, my dream is to one day take exactly what I need for every trip and nothing more. But doing that takes planning, the right luggage, check lists and knowing your itinerary.

Luggage

The luggage you use depends on your travel schedule and your needs. Luggage has changed drastically over the years to accommodate all kinds of travelers. The biggest advancement is that luggage is now soft-sided, lighter and on wheels.

- Shop around for the best deals but don't overlook quality and durability.
- Consider how frequently you travel and whether most of that travel is by air, train or ship.
- Consider how you will travel once you reach your destination—by rental car, taxi, shuttle bus—and how many bags you will want to carry with you.
- Do you want your luggage to fit in the overhead compartment of an airplane?
- Do you prefer to fold, roll or hang your garments?
- Do you prefer soft-sided or hard-sided luggage?
- Do you prefer to carry your luggage over your shoulder, pull it or hold it by handles?

If you plan to add to your luggage, think about the color, style and function of each piece. You don't have to buy an entire luggage set at one time nor do all the pieces of your luggage have to match or come from the same manufacturer. But determine your needs over time and continue to add.

Duffel bags are making a comeback. They are much lighter and have no frame so tend to carry a lot more. Now duffle bags have wheels and long handles so are equally convenient and generally less expensive than standard luggage.

Identifying your Luggage

All luggage, including your carry-ons, should be well marked with your name, business telephone number and business address. This identification should be on the inside of the luggage as well as the outside.

- Do you realize how many almost identical black suitcases are going around the carousels at airports? If you have one of those bags, use some type of identifier to help yours stand out. Attach a distinctive luggage tag. When my mother comes to visit, we can spot her luggage immediately because of the brightly colored yarn she ties to the handles. Come up with your own creative distinction.
- If you work from your home or are retired, use a company name so it gives the impression it is your place of work instead of your home. Do not advertise your home information.
- It is very important to label both the inside and outside of your luggage because your outside tag could be lost.

- Take old destination tags off your luggage. Don't make it difficult and time consuming for the airlines when they are trying to send your luggage to your final destination.

Locks

With all the changes in security, your luggage cannot be locked when presented for check in. There are specific locks that can be used. One such lock that is accepted and recognized is Travel Sentry. This lock carries a special code which the Transportation Security Administration (TSA) can operate. Only the TSA has the special codes and tools that will allow them to open your lock, inspect the bag and items and then relock and send the luggage on its way and to your final destination.

Laptops

A laptop/notebook is part of most business travelers' luggage. At airports you must remove your laptop, place it in a separate bin and let it go through the conveyor belt for security. Be ready for this at the airport and make it quick and easy to open, unpack and repack. Do not send your laptop through the conveyor belt until you walk through. Keep an eye on all of your valuables. With security at a much higher level at all airports, you may be detained and separated from your luggage.

- The case should be light but well padded and easy to carry.
- Make sure it has a shoulder strap in addition to a briefcase handle.

- Have ample compartments inside the case so all items are secured.
- Carry your laptop fully charged and have adaptors if needed.
- Make sure your laptop is well marked with luggage tags inside and out.
- Place a peel-off label on your laptop lid. If you are delayed in security, it is very easy for someone to pick up a similar computer. Place your name and mailing address on the label and make sure it is visible for people to easily see.
- All portable electronic items must remain off during taxi, takeoff, approach and landing. Flight attendants will advise when you may turn on laptops and other electronic devices upon landing.

Your Traveling Briefcase

Keep it lightweight. There are many professional and attractive nylon shoulder bags for both men and women that are much lighter than the standard hard-sided cases. Carry office supplies that you will need during your trip, including notepads, paper clips, pen, pencils, postage stamps, rubber bands, miniature stapler, staples and tape. Always remember to have plenty of business cards, thank-you notes and a calculator, which can be part of your telephone.   If you need a larger briefcase, then choose one on wheels that will easily fit under the seat in the plane or in the overhead bin. These carts on wheels will avoid the wear and tear on your shoulder and back caused by carrying a much too heavy shoulder bag.

How Much to Pack

Do you pack so much that you are not enjoying your travels? If so, you need to repack. I love to bring a lot of clothes and I think it is very important to always appear fresh, well dressed and professional. But there are ways to work around a lot of baggage, look good and still have enough clothes. Here are a few secrets:

- Always pack your hanging clothes in plastic bags before you put them in a garment bag.
- Always put your shoes in bags to protect them.
- Put socks and underclothes inside the shoes or in empty corners.
- The key is to bring basic colors so you can mix and match. A basic top or shirt can be reused with different jackets, and jewelry or scarves can change the look of an outfit and give you two for the space of one.
- Layer-pack your garment bag. Start with a blouse or shirt on a hanger, put a dress or sweater over it and then put a jacket on top. Enclose all in a plastic bag. (More on this later in the chapter.)
- A few basic shoes will do instead of eight or nine pair, which, I admit, I have carried before I wised up.

Problems with Overpacking

- You don't want to leave anything behind.
- You are afraid you won't have enough clothes.
- You aren't sure how to dress or what the weather will be, so you bring extra outfits just in case.
- You threw your clothes together the day of the trip or maybe just hours before you left for the airport.
- You forgot to go to the cleaners so you don't have

113

exactly what you need.

- You pack an iron and a hair dryer when the hotel has them in the room for you. If in doubt, call the hotel to ask if these items are provided, so you can leave yours at home.

To Carry On or to Check?

Some people would never consider checking their bags. For them one good carry-on will do. For others, it would never work. You now need to consider the 3-1-1 rule and make sure all toiletry items are under three ounces, in one-quart zip lock bags and only one carry-on bag. This can be limiting and you might need to check your bag.

- There are all kinds of carry-ons. A carry-on garment bag works great to keep your suits and dresses hanging and you can put other necessities in the pockets. Garment bags will not fit under your seat but they will fit in the overhead bin or in the front of the cabin.
- Probably the most popular carry-on is a suitcase with wheels. The only problem is that some people make them so full and heavy that they struggle to pick them up and put them in the overhead compartment or they are bulging so much, they won't fit. The normal size is 45 linear inches (length + width + height) and no more than 40 to 50 pounds for the overhead bin or under your seat. Sometimes the dimensions and weight will vary with airlines, so check before you pack for that next trip. Exceeding these dimensions or weight specifications can result in a fine that must be paid before leaving for the trip. International and domestic travel has different requirements for number

of carry-on bags, weight and size. Each country is even different, so be prepared and pack light.

- Other carry-ons include duffel bags, totes and travel packs. They can all work, depending on what and how much you plan to put inside.

- Remember the space at your feet is yours but the space over your head is shared. People do become possessive of the overhead space. So when your row is called to board the plane, you might want to be up front to secure that space. Put your bags above your seat. Don't take up another passenger's space just so it is easier for you to grab your bag in the front of the plane when you are deplaning.

- Each airline has rules regarding acceptable items that may be taken on a plane either as a carry-on or with checked luggage. It is advisable to check in advance rather than to have an item confiscated or held for your return. All of this information can be checked at the airlines' web sites.

- You also should consider how you will carry your luggage after you leave the plane, bus or train. You want convenience and ease.

3-1-1 for Carry-On

- Saying all this, you must remember the requirements of 3-1-1 for your carry-ons as established by the Transportation Security Administration (TSA).

- The 3 means all liquids must be in 3 ounce bottles or less. If one of your bottles or containers exceeds 3 ounces, they will confiscate them from you. Do not use a 6-ounce container that may only have 3 ounces of liquid or less. That does not work; they will take it from you.

- The 1 means a one-quart sized, clear, plastic, zip-top bag to hold these items.
- And the last 1 is that you are allowed only one bag per person with these items.
- You must consolidate all your liquids or bottles in the one-quart bag and then place them in a bin for screening in the security process.
- Be prepared. If TSA needs to search your bag it slows down the security line. You also risk the chance of a security check of you, your purse or briefcase. There are TSA or other officials at the security checkpoints reminding you to remove these one quart bags and to place them in a bin. Even if you are in total compliance with 3-1-1, you still might go through a check if the process is held up in any fashion.
- Prescription medications, baby formula and milk are allowed in quantities exceeding three ounces and are not required to be in the zip-top bag. Declare these items for inspection at the checkpoint. Do not expect any other exceptions to the 3-1-1 rule.
- If you have any questions you can check the Web site at http://www.tsa.gov/311 or information under the Transportation Security Administration. This Web site provides details on duty-free items, European security measures, traveling with disabilities or medical conditions, traveling with children and much more.
- Arrive early for your flight and be patient.

Suggested Items for Your Carry-on

- Breakables
- Camera and film
- Clothing (change of underclothes)
- Keys
- Laptop or other electronic equipment
- Medicines and prescriptions
- Personal documents
- Snacks and bottled water. Bottled water or any other drink cannot be taken through security. It must be purchased once you are inside the secured area. Certain exceptions are permissible for baby formula and milk. Check with the Transportation Security Administration before packing or leaving for the airport. It can be costly and inconvenient to lose these items.
- Toiletries (toothbrush, toothpaste, deodorant)
- Valuables (jewelry and cash)
- Work materials

Packing Strategies

From the time you start to plan your trip or receive the first itinerary for a convention or meeting, you need to start preparing what you will take. Consider the weather, the dress codes, schedule of activities and the purpose of your trip.

- Will the dress code be casual, business casual, business or formal or a combination of all of this? The advance information may specify no jeans or shorts. So plan your wardrobe accordingly.

- When I receive the itinerary, I always make an extra copy and write beside each event or program what I will wear, including my shoes, jewelry and belts. When I pull my clothes, I do it by outfits. That way, I don't forget my belt, earrings or other accessories.

- For a four-day meeting with seminars each day and activities each night, you need eight outfits. You don't need to pack eight different outfits but possibly only five basics that can be mixed and matched to give you eight different looks. If you plan to wear slacks to all events, instead of packing eight pairs of pants, pack three or four and be creative. Make selections that can be dressed up or down. It becomes fun and, I promise, you will look different each time.

- Men have it a little easier but not much. A few pair of basic pants, some shirts, jackets, basic shoes and belts, and you are ready to go. But don't take it too lightly. Your dress and appearance are important, too. So the rules still apply to you. Stick to basic colors for the base outfits, shoes and belts and then just build around them.

- A caution to both men and women is that not all clothes mix and match well. Watch your fabrics, weights and colors. Some items just will not work.

- Don't forget to decide what you will wear for your travel days. If you need to go straight to your business meeting, women should wear a knit or material that travels well and men should choose slacks that won't show every wrinkle. Or you may need to take a carry-on bag and change before going to your meeting.

Accessories

- Simple is beautiful. Pack smart and minimize the jewelry you carry. Again, if you stick to two or three basic colors for your wardrobe, fewer accessories will be needed.
- Be very careful about jewelry when you travel. You risk losing your jewelry, leaving it behind or having it stolen. Sometimes when you return to your room between meetings or events, you change quickly and open your jewelry pouch. You could drop something or inadvertently forget to put it away.
- Find jewelry that can be worn with most of your outfits or pack jewelry that can be replaced easily if something should happen.
- Unless you never take them off, don't travel with heirlooms, antiques or sentimental items.
- Many hotels have safes in the rooms. Use it or check with the front desk or concierge and ask to use their safe. The disadvantage is having to ask them repeatedly to open the safe to retrieve an item or to store something.

Preparation List

Don't wait until the last minute to prepare for a trip. Some travel will need more attention and preparation, particularly international trips. Planning ahead will allow you to leave on time and be relaxed and ready for the travel and the actual business part of the trip.

- Pick up your clothes from the dry cleaner.
- Do laundry.

- Replenish your toiletries kits.
- Have ample money and foreign currency if needed.
- Make sure you have enough small bills for tipping at the airport and the hotel.
- Secure luggage tags on your luggage inside and out.
- Get tissue paper and plastic bags to wrap your clothes so they arrive crisp and unwrinkled.
- Don't forget extra resealable bags to hold toiletries or wet clothes like a bathing suit.
- Make sure you are aware of the limits for your luggage including number of bags, size and weight.
- If traveling internationally know what you are allowed to bring in and out of that country.

Several days before I leave on a trip, I put my luggage in my walk-in closet so I can place my travel kits on the bottom and start placing items little by little, so packing is not a chore.

Ready to Roll or Fold

Everyone has preferences in packing. I use a little bit of everything. I'm not a big roller except for my T-shirts or casual clothes. The rest I just fold or hang. Do whatever works best for you and the type of luggage you use. Here are some pointers:

- Rolling works for both light and heavy clothing and is really great for a duffle bag. Just lay the item face down and fold in the sleeves. Then start at the bottom and roll up. Keep the article nice and smooth as you roll, so you are not creating wrinkles. The collar will be on the outside of the roll. You can roll anything. If you have a pair of slacks or jeans, just hold them by the cuffs and lay them down. Make sure you get out all the wrinkles. Then just start to roll up from the cuffs. You may want to pad more delicate items like blouses, shirts, skirts or dresses, with plastic bags or tissue paper and then roll. If something is flimsy, fold it in half lengthwise over another garment to pad the crease and roll them together.

- Interlocking fold means the clothes interlock. First lay down a skirt or a pair of slacks across an open suitcase from top to bottom. Then place a sweater on top of the pants or skirt but place it left to right. Allow the arms of the sweater to drape over the sides of the suitcase. Take the top part of the slacks or skirt and put it over the top of the sweater. Fold the sweater arms in over this and then fold the bottom part of the sweater and bottom part of the slacks or skirt over everything. Now you have a very neat little stack of clothes. You can repeat this process as many times as you wish and, I promise, your clothes will be wrinkle-free. You will have a lot of space along the sides and in the corners to place your underwear, socks and shoes. Remember to stuff those shoes and keep them in bags. Stuffing your shoes will not only save space but also keep the shape of your shoes.

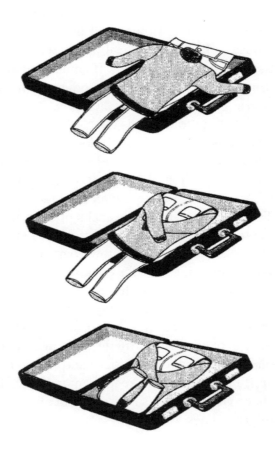

- Many people use a systematic, chronological approach and it is a tremendous time-saver. You can roll or fold but you place your clothes in the suitcase in the order you will wear them. So the first day's clothes will be on the top and the second day will be next. What a great time-saver when you reach your destination, but you must be organized when you pack. I think this is a grand idea, but I like to unpack my clothes when I reach my hotel room even if I am staying only two days. If it is just an overnight trip, I will likely leave my clothes in the suitcase since there are so few items.

Getting the Hang of Garment Bags

I prefer garment bags because as soon as I get to the hotel, I like to take my clothes out and hang them in the closet. Use lots of plastic bags and tissue paper. You can put a dry cleaner's bag over the hanger first to give it a little cushioning and then cover the garments with another plastic bag.

- If I am taking a blouse, I stuff the sleeves with tissue paper to keep them from creasing, the more padding the better. Use hangers that have slight padding so your clothes will not slip off. There is nothing worse than getting to your destination and finding all your clothes at the bottom of the bag.
- When you place your items in the garment bag, start with the longest on the bottom, your more delicate items in the middle and then the remaining items on top. Even though they are all in plastic bags, add a few more bags before closing the zipper. This will provide additional padding and protect the top clothes from the zipper or straps. The bags do not take up a lot of space but provide the necessary padding and prevent wrinkles. They also help in rainy weather and protect your clothing. In addition, I highly recommend placing plastic in the base and top of your suitcase to protect your clothes from rainy weather.

- A space-saving trick is layering or stacking your clothes on hangers. Start by placing a blouse or T-shirt on a hanger. Then add your dress or jacket. Obviously, it would be great to stack actual outfits so they will be ready to go. Remember the plastic bags and tissue paper. If you have a pair of slacks, cover the pant hanger bar with a T-shirt or sweater first and then lay the pants over that to prevent a sharp crease in the pants. You can add a tie over the pants. On top of all of this can go a shirt and a jacket. When you reach the hotel, you can place the clothes on individual hangers provided by the hotel.
- I do not recommend putting toiletries in a garment bag. If it is tossed or thrown to the ground, the chances are a lot greater that items could burst, leak or spill. Also do not place anything of value in the outside pockets of a garment bag. Since locking these bags is more difficult, it is just not safe.
- Some airlines will provide a garment bag box to be checked if you request one. But when they are really busy, they do not want to take the time to assemble one and have you place your garment bag inside. Still, it is worth asking. Make sure you print your name clearly on the outside of the box on both sides. These boxes are becoming harder and harder to find. More likely they will place your garment bag (or ask them to do it) into a bin. That helps a lot.
- I highly recommend that you purchase a garment bag that is on wheels.

Ties

There is nothing worse than a tie that is badly wrinkled. One way to prevent wrinkles is to roll ties and place them in a jacket pocket.

You can also lay them flat inside the sleeve of a jacket or lay them over the pants on the hanger bar. Carrying cases made especially for ties are great for travelers (and a good gift for the guy who has everything).

Travel Toiletries Kits

I have three kits that are always packed and ready to go. One I hook on the back of the door in the bathroom as soon as I arrive; it holds my toothpaste and all those necessary items. Another kit holds all my hair items including a comb, brush, small mirror and my hair dryer, if I need one. The last one keeps my other toiletries all in plastic bags. As soon as I return from a trip, I replenish each of these bags and keep them with my suitcases. I just move them to whatever suitcase I am taking for the next trip and I am ready to go. Hotels provide some amenities such as shampoo and conditioner. If you prefer particular brands, then pack your own in travel sizes. Here is an inventory of items for your travel kits:

Aspirin	Moisturizer
Comb and brush	Mouthwash
Conditioner	Nail supplies
Contact lens supplies	Razor
Cotton swabs/balls	Safety pins
Dental floss	Sewing kit
Deodorant	Shampoo
Facial cream/cleanser	Shaving cream
First-aid kit	Spot remover
Hair dryer	Sunscreen
Hairspray	Tissues
Hand lotion	Toothbrush
Insect repellent	Toothpaste
Makeup	Tweezers
Makeup remover	Wipes
Woolite (or small bottle of detergent)	

If you purchase small plastic bottles to fill with your products, remember not to fill them to the top. The changes in air pressure during a flight could cause containers to leak. Put all of these items in a resealable bag. Remember the 3-1-1 rule at the airport if you plan to carry any of these on board.

Checklists

When I started preparing this book, I asked several people for checklists and received many great samples. But the best one came from my friend Laurie Sprouse. It was the most complete list I had ever seen. So, with my gratitude, here is Laurie's list, with just a few adjustments:

Documents

AAA card
Airline tickets
Check receipt
Copy of documents
Driver's license
Health insurance card

Itinerary
Passport
  (and a copy of the front page)
Rental car voucher
Train tickets
Visa

Money
Cash (small bills for tipping)
Credit cards (copy of the front and back of cards)
Foreign currency
Traveler's checks

Miscellaneous
Appointment information/Electronic equipment
  (names, addresses, phone numbers)
Electrical adapter for international use
Communication equipment – cell phones, laptops, etc.
Calling cards/dialing information
Personal phone numbers and addresses

Business Collateral
Brochures
Business cards
Business gifts
Information packets
Picture book
CDs/DVDs/iPods

Carry-ons
Airplane pillow
Aspirin
Bottled water
Cell phone
Ear plugs/mask
Sleeping pills

Computer
Adaptor	E-mail information
Car adaptor	Extra battery
CDs/DVDs/iPods	Fax modem
Cord	Phone line/adapters

iPods or Similar Equipment
Batteries (extended battery)
Songs and Videos

Books/Maps
Guide books
Phrase book
Reading materials
Road maps

Supplies
Business note paper
Calculator
Envelopes
Expense report forms
File folders
Highlighters
Notepads
Paperclips
Pens, staplers, staples
Rubber bands
Stamps
Thank-you notes

Clothing
Bathing suit/cover-up
Belts/suspenders
Business suits/dresses
Coat/jacket/raincoat
Formal/cocktail attire
Golf attire (if needed)
Handkerchiefs
Jackets/sport coat
Jeans/shorts
Jewelry/accessories
Rain jacket
Shirts (dress, casual)
Shoes (business, casual, athletic)
Slacks (dress, casual)
Sleepwear/slippers
Socks/hosiery
Sweaters/turtlenecks
Ties/scarves
Underwear
Work-out gear

Cold Weather

Gloves
Hat/ski headband
Overcoat
Rain jacket

Scarf
Sweater
Thermals

Personal

Artificial sweetener
Chewing gum/mints
Curling iron and adapter
Eye/contact solutions
Face lotions
Hair dryer and adapter
Ibuprofen/aspirin
Snacks

Sunglasses
Tea/hot chocolate
Travel toiletries kits
Umbrella
Vitamins, herbs, cold
  medications
Prescriptions in original bottles

Notes for Traveling Abroad

- Have an up-to-date passport. Be sure it will be valid when you are ready to return home. It can take four to five weeks to receive a new passport and three to four weeks to renew one. If you don't have this much time, you can visit a U.S. Passport Office and they will handle your request for an additional fee.
- Passports are now required for travel to Canada and Mexico.
- Be aware of any visas you may need.
- Do you need any inoculations for your destination? Plan this well in advance. It may take weeks to receive all the necessary shots.
- It is essential to purchase electrical adapters before you leave on an international trip. Most countries use a standard 220-volt current, but in the United States and Canada, we use 110 volts. You can find adapters in any travel store or in most major department stores.
- Keep all documents together in a pouch or a travel case that you always have with you. These should include your passport, visa, copies of your prescriptions, traveler's checks, credit card numbers and important phone numbers. It is highly recommended that you also keep a copy of the first page of your passport and credit card information in another secured place and one back in your office. These are critical items and when you carry them, keep them close to your body and concealed.

Shipping Luggage

At times, I will have back-to-back business trips. Of course, they inevitably will be different types of trips to different climates. You can ship luggage to your hotel via a parcel service like UPS or FedEx. Allow enough time for it to arrive ahead of you and alert the hotel to be expecting it. The hotel can store it and have it waiting for you upon arrival. It is so convenient and so easy. You can also ship home a box of convention/trade show materials, gifts or a suitcase of laundry to avoid having to check or carry extra baggage on your return trip.

While You're Gone

Review the tips in Chapter Fourteen "Being Safe at Home and on the Road." Don't forget about your mail, newspapers, keeping lights on and giving the impression that you are still at home. Trust a neighbor or a good friend to keep an eye on your home or apartment. Also remember to use the "Out of Office" function on your computer to provide information about how you may be reached.

The point is . . .
Efficient packing means knowing how and what to pack as well as using the right luggage for the trip. Checklists and systems help simplify your business trips. The new security rules can make a difference so keep up-to-date on all rules and regulations.

TWELVE

What Happened to the Friendly Skies? Airplane, Airport Etiquette

●—●—●—●—●—●—●—●

Flying is a great and convenient way to get from point A to point B. But it can be a challenge and unpleasant when people around you are not on their airline best. Whether we are flying for professional or personal pleasure, there are a few things we need to think about every time we enter an airport and take a flight.

Courtesy, respect and consideration sure are nice when you sit within inches of your new best friend. Your flight may be less than a hour, or you may be in transit for hours or days. The flight attendants do their best and everything they possibly can to accommodate you, but we, as passengers, also need to help make flying more enjoyable and relaxing and a much better experience.

- **Going Through Security – Be Ready**
  Don't wait until you are at the conveyer belt to start to get ready. If you have a laptop, take it out of the case and put it in a separate bin. My advice is to also put some identification on the top of your laptop. A small sticky label with at least your name is advisable. Laptops are like black suitcases, they all look alike at the other end of the conveyer belt.

  Ninety-nine percent of shoes will need to come off. It is a lot easier to take them off than to go through security again or to be patted down by security. Some airports even have booties you can slip on so your feet don't get cold or dirty.

Move away from the conveyor as quickly as possible when your items come off. Don't stop to put your shoes back on or to load up your computer. Gather everything and move to the end of the conveyor or completely out of the way. Allow the people behind you space and easy access to collect their items. Hopefully they will move along quickly too.

- **Sitting in the Lobby Waiting for Your Flight**
  To my knowledge most people only need one seat to sit down. Don't take one seat for you, one for your briefcase, and one for your meal. Share.

  I enjoy walking up to a person occupying three seats and asking them if I can sit next to them. It forces them to move their lunch off the seat or their newspaper. It is rude on their part, especially if there are elderly people standing or families with small children.

- **Getting on the Plane**
  Get to your seat and move in. Do not block the aisle, and do not stop to put your luggage above Seat 5C when you are sitting in 25C. That's their space, not yours, so go use your own. Remember, the foot space under your seat in front of you is yours, but the overhead is a shared, communal area.

- **Phones**
  Turn your phone off when asked by the flight attendants. Do not scream when you are allowed to use them. Everyone throughout the plane does not need to know about your family vacation or where your partner needs to meet you.

Be considerate of the people around you. Trust me, cell phones and all technology have advanced beyond needing to scream into the phone. Avoid the "cell yell."

- **Laptops, iPods and Games**
  Remember, electronic devices do make noise. It can be annoying if you use your laptop or play noisy games the whole way to Europe. There are sound controls on games and DVDs, so please use them. Laptops do vibrate, and could bounce the seat in front of you. People around you may not want to rock and roll to the bass of your music. Some airlines only allow games that have headsets, so come prepared. Children need games and toys to keep them content during the flight, but do not make them the noisiest ones they own. Nice quiet games and toys work, too. Remember to bring your head sets and save the fees that airlines are now charging for their headsets.

- **Snack Trays and Reclining**
  When you hear the announcement that you are free to recline your seats and use your snack trays, be gentle. You do not want to bounce around the person in front of you by quickly moving those trays up and down. Nor do you need to recline so fast or far that it is a tremendous inconvenience to the person behind you. Go back easy, and allow that person a few seconds to prepare for your trip into their lap.

  If you are traveling with children, please be aware if they are moving the snack trays up and down and kicking the back of the seat. That gets old real fast.

- **Speaking of Whiplash**
  When you get out of your seat during the flight, use
  your armrest to push yourself up or to get back into your
  seat. Do not grab the back of the seat in front of you.
  When you use the back of their seat, you are pulling them
  back, possibly waking them up from a nice nap and even
  grabbing their hair.

- **Chatty Cathy or Talkative Tom**
  A lot of people really do not want to become best
  friends with the people sitting next to them on the plane. So
  take hints if they continue to read or look out
  the window. It is nice to introduce yourself when you are
  first seated and hopefully you will decide if they want to
  chat or just stay in their own zone. Honor that request.

  If that person continues to talk, you might say, "I would
  love to talk but I have a deadline and really need to get this
  project completed by the time I reach the city." Or
  even, "Please excuse me but I really need to work on my
  presentation for my meeting when I get to the city."
  But if you are not working and just reading a book then,
  "I am so close to the end of this book and I really can't
  put it down." If none of these work then just pretend
  you are sleeping.

- **Watch Those Bags on Your Shoulder**
  When you are moving back the aisle getting on the plane,
  watch those bags you are carrying on your shoulder. They
  can be painful when you swing or turn and hit someone as
  you go by.

- **The Overhead Bins**
  You do not have to run up and down the aisles assisting shorter or elderly people trying to put their bags in the overhead compartments. But if you are right there, help them out. It moves things along and can be your good deed for the day.

- **Bathroom Breaks**
  Try and be considerate. If you are in a middle seat or the window seat, try to get up and use the bathroom when your other seat partners are still awake or possibly when one of them also gets up, you can follow them. Don't let them go to the bathroom, come back and get all situated and then ask to get past them. If you also see that your seat partner is getting ready to set up their computer, you might want to try and get to the rest room before they are all set up.

  Airlines are now requesting that you only use the rest room in your class of the airplane. Don't try and beat the system and use the rest room in first class if you are in coach class.

- **Wait Your Turn**
  When it is time to exit the plane, wait your turn. Do not come rushing and pushing from the back to get ahead. Go seat-by-seat, row-by-row.

  If planes are delayed and arriving late to the airport, generally the flight attendants will ask all passengers to stay seated if they are not on connecting flights. Let those passengers trying to catch another flight depart the plane.

Don't pretend that you have a connecting flight and get off with them. Chances are your luggage won't be there anyway.

- **Dress Nice**
  I remember when the standard dress for flying was strictly business. The men wore suits and the women wore dresses and panty hose. My first trip to Europe was in a dress, low heels and panty hose. It was just the style of dress. Now people look like they literally got out of bed and came directly to the airport. You don't need to be in full business garb but at least come prepared to come in contact with other people. You never know who you might meet sitting in the lobby of an airport or on the plane. I have even booked business with people I have met during my travels.

Flying can be fun and a lot of us do it daily, so give it your best etiquette. It might even make the flight a little more enjoyable. (See Chapter Fourteen on "Being Safe at Home and on the Road.")

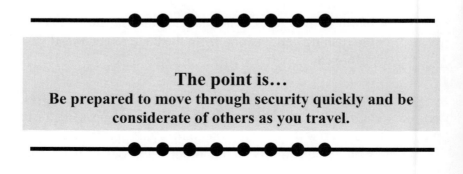

The point is...
Be prepared to move through security quickly and be considerate of others as you travel.

THIRTEEN

Public Etiquette

Public etiquette is required every day and applies to total strangers—people that we will probably never see again or possibly people in the building where we work, bank, shop or take our children to school. Wouldn't it be nice if people would hold a door for you, allow you to cut into traffic as you are pulling onto a street as you are driving or allow you to get out of the elevator before they try to squeeze in? Public etiquette generally can take a matter of a few seconds but the end result can make your day.

- **Elevators**
  Let people out before you try to enter an elevator. Even teach young children to wait their turn. If you let the people exit, the system works a lot better. If you see elderly people or someone who needs assistance, step aside and hold the door for them and then enter the elevator. As you enter the elevator try to move back as far as possible. If you are getting off on the next floor, then at least move to the side. If you have a lot of luggage, you might want to wait for the next elevator instead of running over everyone's toes as you enter.

- **Escalators**
  The etiquette on downward escalators is for the man to go on first in case a woman or child should fall, they could break the fall or help them. If you are approaching the same time as another person, consider

their age or situation. Do they have smaller children or possibly needs a little assistance? Allow them to go before you.

- **Holding Doors**
  As you enter a room or a building, always turn to see if someone is close behind you and will be entering the same area. If so, hesitate for a second and hold the door for them. It doesn't matter their age or gender, just be kind and hold the door. If someone holds the door for you, a nice smile and thank-you would be appropriate and appreciated.

- **Cars**
  Allow people to change lanes, come on to the road from an exit or pull out. Again, it might be a matter of a few seconds so be courteous as you drive. Of course, it would be nice if the person that you just let squeeze in ahead of you would raise their hand to say thank-you.

- **Parking Spaces**
  Use your turn signal if you are ready to pull into a parking spot.

- **Drive-Through Windows, Check-Outs, Fast Foods**
  The people on the other side of that window or the counter are basically on their feet for their shift and have to meet and greet people all day. It would be truly appreciated if you could give them a nice smile and hello instead of being on your cell phone or listening to your iPod or radio.

- **Open Space**
  Don't stop in the middle of a space and block other people. This includes as you are exiting a room, entering a hallway, stopping in the middle of a sidewalk or even leaving your shopping cart right in the middle of the aisle as you decide on your next meal. Just look around and move to the side. Allow people to get by. Even as you are walking down a sidewalk the passage is the same as you drive. Move to the right and allow people to pass to your left. But if you are in another country, remember which side of the road they are driving. They, too, walk the same as they drive. So you may need to move to the left instead of right.

  Also be careful with umbrellas. As you pass people slightly turn your umbrella away from them so you are not dripping additional raindrops on them.

- **Giving Up Your Seat**
  Before you get too comfy in that last seat on the subway, tram or train or in a waiting area, just make sure there is not someone that needs that seat more than you. It could be an elderly person, a person with a physical challenge who would be more comfortable sitting down or even a mother with a child. At least offer your seat. If they decline your offer, then enjoy your ride.

- **In Line and Your Friends**
  Be careful when you are in a long line waiting to get tickets, enter a building or even a ride and a few of your friends come up and want to jump the line and

get in front of many other people. If they don't want to move to their proper position, then you could even offer to go to the end of line with them. Hopefully that would convince them to go the end of the line.

Public etiquette should be a habit and not a task. Just think how you would like to be treated and return the favor.

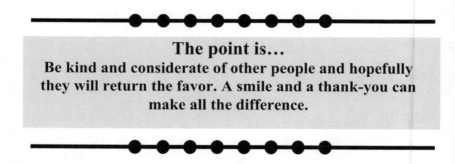

The point is...
Be kind and considerate of other people and hopefully they will return the favor. A smile and a thank-you can make all the difference.

FOURTEEN

Being Safe at Home and on The Road

————————— ● ● ● ● ● ● ● —————————

Personal safety and security is important to everyone. After all, if you and your loved ones are not safe, nothing else matters much, does it? "It can't happen here" is an excuse that is not applicable anymore. You can be unsafe at work, on the road and in your own home. No area—and no one—is exempt. Sometimes your instincts help protect you, but at all times, it pays to practice well-thought-out routines to ensure you are doing your reasonable best to avoid situations that may put you in danger or make you a victim of crime.

General Rules

- Stay alert and tuned in to your surroundings. Don't be taken by surprise. Be aware and be prepared.
- Walk confidently. Don't show fear. Don't look like a victim.
- Trust your instincts. If you feel uncomfortable in a place or situation, leave right away and get help if necessary.
- Choose busy streets and avoid going through vacant lots, alleys or other deserted areas. At night, walk in well-lighted areas whenever possible.
- Always lock your car and take the keys, even if you will be gone only a short time.
- If you are coming or going after dark, park in a well-lighted area that still will be well lighted when you return.
- Be especially alert when using enclosed parking garages. Don't walk into an area if you feel uncomfortable. Ask a

security person to escort you; it's their job.
- Leave only your ignition key with a parking attendant. Don't leave your house key or other keys on the key ring.

ATM Machines

- Try to plan your ATM visits during the day.
- Choose an ATM location in a busy public place. Avoid making withdrawals in isolated areas.
- When you finish, place the money in your purse or wallet and leave as soon as possible.
- Watch for suspicious people waiting around an ATM.
- When using a drive-through ATM, keep your doors locked and be prepared to drive away quickly. If anyone approaches your car on foot, roll up your window and drive away. If you have not finished your transaction, press the "cancel" button, retrieve your card and leave quickly.

Home and Apartment Safety

- Make sure your home is safe. If you forgot your key, can you get in? If you can, so can a burglar.
- Make sure your windows, especially at ground level, have good locks—and use them.
- Don't tempt burglars. Leaving shades or draperies open helps them spot items of value.
- Make sure porches and other possible entrances are well lighted.
- Never leave a note in the door for anyone explaining why you are not at home.

- Trim any bushes or trees that hide doors or windows. Keep ladders, tools, toys and recreational equipment inside when you are not using them.
- Don't hide your house keys under the doormat or in a flowerpot. It is much wiser to give an extra key to a trusted neighbor.
- Always close and lock garage doors.
- Place just your last name on the mailbox. Never provide marital status or first or middle name on your nameplate or mailbox.
- Ask a trusted neighbor to collect your mail and newspapers when you are traveling and offer to return the favor. Leave word about when you are leaving, when you will return and how you can be reached in an emergency. Or cancel your paper and have the post office hold your mail until you return. This is any easy process and can be handled on-line or by phone. Don't leave the papers accumulating in the driveway or the mail overflowing in your mail box.
- Put automatic timers on at least two lights and possibly a radio to help your home look and sound occupied.
- Keep written records of all furniture, jewelry and electronic products. If possible, keep these records in a safe-deposit box, fireproof safe or other secure area.
- Replace or re-key locks when moving into an apartment or previously owned home.
- If you live in an apartment, make sure that entrances, parking areas, hallways, stairways, laundry rooms and other common areas are well lighted. Report burned out bulbs or other problems to the manager.
- Make sure fire stairs are locked from the stairwell side, with an emergency exit at ground level.
- Laundry rooms and storage areas should always be kept locked unless a resident is actually inside.

145

Telephone Safety

- Never give personal information (e.g., name, age, address) to a stranger on the telephone.
- Never reveal when you will or will not be home or that you are home alone.
- Instruct babysitters never to tell anyone who calls that they are home alone with children.
- Instruct children to say, "My mom can't come to the phone now. May I take a message?" instead of indicating they are home alone.
- If possible, have your calls forwarded while you are out of town or check your messages regularly.
- Do not leave a message on your recorder that you away or on vacation for a given amount of time. You have given burglars the ideal time to visit your home.

Car Safety

- As soon as you enter your car, lock the doors. Then get all your items situated and do whatever you need to do sitting in a safe area.
- If you have children, get them in the car and lock the doors. Be aware of your surroundings. Someone could approach your car while you are taking care of the kids and car seats.
- Always lock your car doors while driving and roll windows up far enough to keep anyone from reaching inside.
- At stop signs and lights, keep the car in gear and stay alert.
- Travel well-lighted, busy streets. You can spare the extra

minutes it may take to avoid unsafe areas.

- Keep your purse and other valuables out of sight, even when you are driving in your locked car.
- Park in safe, well-lighted areas near your destination.
- When you arrive home, leave your headlights on until you have the car in the garage. Stay in your car and use your remote control garage door opener to lock the garage door. Then exit your car.
- Don't hide spare keys. They can be found.
- If your car breaks down, use your cell phone to call for roadside assistance. You should also raise the hood and place emergency reflectors or flares on the road. Tie a handkerchief to the aerial or door handle. Then stay in the locked car. When someone stops to help, don't get out. Ask him or her, through a closed or cracked window, to telephone the police to come and help. Likewise, if you see a stranded motorist, it is better not to stop. Advise them you will be calling the police to provide assistance.
- If you think you are being followed, do not drive to your home, revealing where you live. Stay calm, think clearly and control the situation. Flash your lights and sound your horn long enough to attract attention to yourself and, consequently, the person following you. Drive to a fire station, a police station or a busy, well-lighted retail area, anywhere there will be people and you will feel safe. Continue sounding your horn and flashing your lights. Do not leave the safe location until you are sure the follower is gone. Use your cell phone to call 911.

Rental Cars

- Don't announce that you are a tourist, are driving a rental car or are totally lost.
- Make sure your rental car is not easily identified as a rental.
- Prepare your route before leaving the rental office or airport lot.
- Invest a little more money to get a car with a global positioning system (GPS) or navigation system to help prevent your getting lost in an unfamiliar city.
- Try to pick up and return rental cars during daylight hours or when there are people around.
- Keep your luggage in the trunk and your purse/briefcase out of reach and out of sight.
- Always lock the doors and be aware of your surroundings when you get in and out of your car.

Hotel Safety

- Call in advance to ask about the location of the hotel, nearby restaurants and the surrounding area.
- When you enter a hotel, be aware of your surroundings.
- When you register, keep your personal belongings within your range and view.
- Never leave your credit card out for someone to see your name or credit card numbers.
- Have cash available to tip in your pocket or easy to grab. Avoid opening your purse or wallet and exposing all your credit cards and/or cash.

- Make sure your room number is never given out or announced. The front desk can just show you the room number on the folder or key card. If the bellman asks your room number, again just show him. Do not make your room number public. If your room number is given out, ask to change rooms and tell the clerk not to mention the number.
- Have your room key or card out as you walk to your room. Be ready to enter your room instantly. Never carry so much in your hands that you cannot get into your room quickly.
- Avoid rooms around corners or in dark areas. If you are uncomfortable with the placement of your room, ask to have it changed.
- If there is a sliding door, make sure it has a safety lock and metal bar. If you are on the first floor and feel uncomfortable, ask to be moved to an upper level.
- The ideal room is between the second and seventh floor, avoiding the ground floor but giving you less distance to cover in case of fire and within range of fire equipment reach.
- When you enter the room, check the entire area while the bellman is still in the room with you. This includes the closet and the bathroom. You don't have to be obvious, just careful.
- Be aware of the exits on your floor. Make sure the exit doors and routes to them are indicated by illuminated signs.
- Be sure your room has a fire alarm system and a sprinkler system.
- Keep your room key and valuables handy in case you need to leave the room quickly for a fire alarm.
- Once you are in the room, immediately lock the door and

secure the deadbolt. Make this a habit.

- Do not use the latch lock to keep the door open while you run out to get ice or a cold drink. A person could enter your room within that instant.
- Be aware of your surroundings while you are in the hall. If you feel uncomfortable, let hotel security know. Have someone walk you to your room, the parking garage or your meeting.
- If a room safe is available, use it, or ask the front desk for assistance in securing your valuables.
- When you leave your room, do not put the sign on your door for the maid to clean your room, announcing that you are out.
- When you leave your room, keep the television or radio on low and keep a light on for your return. Always give the impression someone is still in the room.
- Never leave valuable items out and available in your room.
- Make sure your door closes and locks every time you leave. Some doors will not do that automatically.
- If you order food from outside the hotel, have it delivered to the front desk and have hotel staff deliver it to your room. Do not give out your hotel room number to a stranger or anyone not employed by the hotel.
- If the hotel health club does not have an attendant, use the facility only when there are many people around.
- Use valet parking. It may cost more but it is safer, especially if you arrive late and need to walk through a dark parking lot or garage.

Airline Safety

- Give yourself plenty of time to check in and to go through security points due to the heightened security precautions at airports. Time recommendations will vary but most airports suggest you arrive 90 minutes before domestic flight departures when you are checking your luggage and 60 minutes before departure if you will have just carry-ons. For international flights, travelers are advised to arrive no less than two hours before departure.
- For all flights it is necessary to have a government-issued photo ID available as well as your ticket or printed itinerary for electronic ticketing.
- Photo identification is now required at both check-in and going through security. Minors must be verified by a parent or guardian.
- For flying internationally, passports are necessary and visas and inoculation information may be required for certain countries.
- If you have a very early morning flight, confirm the ticket counter opening time with the airport to prevent waiting unnecessarily.

Airport Security Checkpoints

- New safety procedures are in place for your safety and the safety of all passengers, so please remember this when security personnel ask you to remove your shoes or boots or to go back through a check point.
- Do not expect any wrapped gifts to go through security. They will be subject to search.

- At security or boarding, your bags may be subjected to a random search or you may have to submit to an electronic wand search.
- Do not leave your bags unattended or ask anyone to watch your bags.

In Flight

- If you have a concern or are alarmed about a passenger(s), immediately notify a flight attendant.
- Recent safety studies recommend verbally confronting a violent, unusual or combative person before attempting to restrain him.
- Do not take it upon yourself to be a hero and react hastily. In any situation, on the ground or in the air, use the best resources you have available before trying to handle a situation on your own. There are now personnel on planes and on the ground who have been trained for these circumstances.

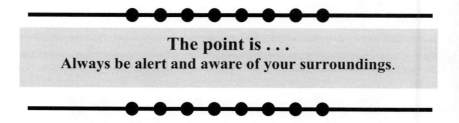

The point is . . .
Always be alert and aware of your surroundings.

FIFTEEN

Tipping Guidelines

How tipping actually started is about as confusing as when, how much and where we should tip. But the biggest question is why people tip. Do we feel we will get better service the next time we visit that establishment, do we want to look like we are big spenders and leave a larger amount of money than necessary or do we just automatically have a set amount and leave that no matter how the service was performed?

Some say tipping started back in the Middle Ages and some argue it first became prominent in bars in England when people would throw money off the table to get better service. The Dutch claim it came from their word "tippen," which came from a coin being tapped on a glass to get a waiter's attention. But some say it is from the Latin word "stips," which means gift. But the origin I like is "To Insure Promptitude." The history states that in a London pub a bowl was marked with these words to encourage people to drop money into the bowl for good service. From the first letters in each of these words the word tip was derived.

No matter how it started, it is growing in magnitude and people will tip billions of dollars annually. Many service people receive more from tips than they are paid in actual salary. But the bottom line should be that we tip according to the services that are provided to us. You may add the tip on your bill and charge the total to your credit card or hotel room. You should always be prepared with smaller bills either in your pocket or a place that is easy for you to reach without exposing all your other cash or credit cards. But if you have insufficient cash, you may ask the person you wish to tip if he has change. If you promise to take care of someone later, make sure to honor that commitment when you have proper change.

Yes, it is fine not to tip when you receive unsatisfactory service or rudeness from a server. But more importantly you need to tell management why they are not being tipped. Unfortunately, some people leave fifteen percent for all services no matter how they are treated. But be careful you do not punish everyone on the tipping line because one person in the link is substandard. Many tips are shared with everyone at the restaurant or establishment. Your food was great and served in a reasonable amount of time, the establishment was clean and every other person was kind except your server. This is when you provide your tip to the manager explaining whom you would like to receive the tip and your disappointment with the server. You don't need to get that person fired, but it needs to be brought to the management's attention.

The suggested guidelines below can vary depending on the city, the type of facility, the frequency of your patronage at that venue and the service that was rendered. These are just starting points and suggested guidelines.

Hotels

- Bellman: If one person carries your luggage from the car or taxi to the registration desk, waits for you and then carries the bags to your room, he should receive no less than $1 per bag; $3 to $4 for several bags. It is more likely that one person will carry your bags from the car to the front desk and a second person will escort you to your room. If this is the case, both people should be tipped. My guideline is $2 for the first bag and $1-$2 for each additional bag. Think ahead and put a few dollars in your pocket or someplace easy to access quickly so you won't expose the contents of your wallet or purse in the hotel lobby.

- Concierge: Just asking a small request of a concierge does not require a tip. But if a concierge performs a special service, such as getting you tickets to the theater or a dinner reservation at the newest restaurant in town, tip $5 to $20 or more if the request took a long time or was difficult to accomplish.

- Doorman: If this person quickly gets you a cab, you may want to tip from $1 to $10, depending on the weather and the number of guests waiting in line. Also, if you arrive at a hotel and ask the doorman to hold your car up front while you go in for lunch or a meeting, then $5 to $20 is appropriate. Always make sure that the amount of the tip is more than what it would have cost you in valet parking. So if valet is $12 to $15 then the minimum would be $20 for them to hold your car.

- Housekeeping: A $2 to $4 per day gratuity can be left on the nightstand, near the bathroom sink or on the bed. You should leave these tips on a daily basis because of shift changes. Envelopes might be left by your housekeepers with their name and how to reach them for additional service. If so then use the envelope or envelopes usually found in the hotel's guest directory folder. If an envelope is not available, then just leave the money. If you are sharing a room, then you should double your tip.

- Parking Garage Attendant: $1 to $2
- Restroom Attendants: Tip $.50 to $1
- Shoe Shine: $1 to $2

- Spa Attendant: Tip $2 if he or she provides towels or services.
- Valet: Charges for valet services will appear on the room bill, but $1 (more if you have more items serviced) is a good delivery tip.
- Valet Parking: $1 to $2 is normal. If the valet holds your car in the front of the building for a very brief time, then $5 to $10 is appropriate; if for an extended period, then $20 is more appropriate.
- Remember, these are just guidelines. You may wish to tip more for good service.

Restaurants

- At a modest restaurant, 15 percent is a good guideline; 20 percent to 25 percent at a more expensive restaurant is standard.
- The maitre d' usually is not tipped but if you are a regular at the restaurant or if he provides you with a great table or helps you with a very important business meal, then $5 to $20 is appropriate.
- The captain or head waiter should be tipped 5 percent of the bill. This can be either in cash or specified on the bill if you use a credit card.
- Servers should be tipped approximately 15 percent to 20 percent of your total bill, according to the level of service provided. Usually this tip is divided among the entire service team, including bartenders and bussing staff.
- The sommelier (wine steward) should be tipped 15 percent of the wine bill. But this is necessary only if the sommelier performs a special service for you and your guests by selecting or assisting with the wine

choices for your meal. This can be extremely costly if you are selecting very expensive wines. Be fair and use your best judgement.

- European Tipping: It is the custom in most European countries to include the tip, or a gratuity of usually 15 percent in the restaurant bill before it is presented. If the service is extraordinary, you can provide an additional tip.

Other Tipping:

- Barbers, Hair Stylists, Masseurs and Manicurists: A tip equivalent to 15 percent to 20 percent of the cost of the service is customary. I am always asked if you should tip the owner of the salon if they do your hair. My answer is yes unless they build the tip into their costs. You can just ask if the tip is included. If they tell you no, then you need to decide what additional tip you would like to leave.

- Cab Drivers: The usual tip is 15 percent to 20 percent of your fare on the meter, plus $1 per bag if the driver loads them in and out of the trunk.

- Check Room Attendants: $1 per coat. Add another dollar for a briefcase, umbrella or any other item.

- Delivery Persons: People who deliver flowers, groceries (whether to your door or your car), meals, fruit baskets, etc., should be tipped $1 to $3, depending on the number or weight and size of the items. Federal Express, DHL, UPS and U.S. Postal Service delivery people are not usually tipped, but a $10 to $20 holiday tip for the regular service provider is appropriate. Trash collectors, newspaper deliverymen, yardmen and other service suppliers may also receive annual holiday gratuities. Be aware of government rules regarding cash being given to their employees. Generally $20 is the maximum they can receive but check on the rules in your area for all delivery service people. Also baked goods work in addition to your monetary gift.

- Fast Food Restaurants: The wait staff that cleans up after your child's birthday party at a fast-food chain or pizza parlor or a person who is standing on the corner in the heat to serve you a hot dog or ice cream deserves a $1 to $3 tip. If you come to a fast-food restaurant with 20 kids for a birthday party, staffers deserve a lot more for their tip. Consider a dollar per child to clean up the mess.

- Golf Caddie: Tip 15 percent to 20 percent of the price of the green fee.

- Luggage Handlers at Airports or Train Stations: At least $1 per checked bag is paid when you receive the claim checks. But now some airlines are charging $2 per bag and the gratuity is not included. So if you have two bags you will pay $4 to the airline just to handle your bags and then another $2 to $3 as the tip.

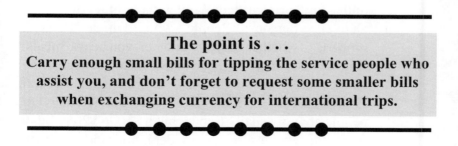

The point is . . .
Carry enough small bills for tipping the service people who assist you, and don't forget to request some smaller bills when exchanging currency for international trips.

SIXTEEN

Business Entertainment, Gifts and RSVPs

Business entertaining can range from a one-on-one luncheon to programs, sporting events or meetings for hundreds of people. The intent when you entertain may be to meet someone for the first time, close a business deal, strengthen a business relationship or sell clients on your company and what you can offer them. If at the end of each function you believe your goal was accomplished, then it was worth your time, your money and the time of your customers.

Individual Entertainment

Even a dinner for one client needs research. You can check with a client's assistant to learn about a favorite restaurant and food or wine preferences. Planning will be appreciated by the client and can make a difference for you and your business.

On a one-on-one basis, you may entertain to:
- Introduce yourself to the client
- Thank someone for a great job or for their business
- Promote your company and products
- Exchange ideas
- Honor an individual or a group on a special occasion

Group Entertainment

Detailed planning is involved when entertaining groups to

showcase your organization or product. Every detail must be covered to make your event a complete success. To get the most from your investment, you must know your audience.

For a two- or three-day event, your planning may include:

- Activities/Tickets (plays, concerts, sporting events)
- Amenities
- Back-up venues for any outside activities
- Budget
- Entertainment (unique, creative and different)
- Flowers/Decorations
- Hotel/Venues
- Invitations/RSVPs
- Itinerary
- Menus (no duplicates during the event)
- Photographers/Videographer
- Press or Security (if needed)
- Sponsors
- Staffing
- Transportation (both air and ground)

Make sure your guests know:
- The complete itinerary you have planned
- The dress code for each part of the event
- If they may bring a guest. If so, be extremely specific about the details.
- Airline details (cancellation/change policies and deadlines)
- Beginning and ending times of the event
- That their participation and attendance is expected and appreciated at all scheduled events and activities.
- That the invitation is non-transferable

Bringing an Extra Person

Never bring a date or a friend to an event or dinner party unless the invitation clearly states "and guest." Especially in the situation of a dinner party, the hosts probably have set only for the invited guests who responded. For you to show up with a guest in tow would be extremely uncomfortable for everyone.

Paying the Bill

- If you invite someone to a luncheon or dinner, you should pick up the bill. As soon as the bill arrives, move it to your side of the table and handle it immediately so there is no confusion or argument over who pays.
- If two business acquaintances frequently dine together as friends, even though some business is discussed, it is perfectly fine to split the bill or take turns picking up the bill.
- If a woman invites a man or several men to lunch to discuss her new project or a business deal, it is appropriate that she pay the bill. It is best that she handles payment ahead of time with the headwaiter or restaurant manager. Then her guests will never see the bill and there will be no discussion.

Arriving for a Business Function

- Punctuality is critical for all business meetings. You should make every effort to arrive a few minutes early for all business meetings. If you arrive ahead of your guest at a restaurant, you should wait a few minutes before going in to sit alone. If you see the restaurant is getting crowded, you may ask to be seated unless the restaurant has a policy of seating only complete parties.

- If several people are invited to lunch, ask to be seated as soon as two people have arrived if the restaurant will accommodate you.
- If you are waiting at the table or a bar for another person or persons, it is completely acceptable to order a beverage before the other person arrives, but you should never order your meal before your guests arrive.
- How long should you wait for a client or customer for a dining meeting? The standard is 30 minutes and then you can either leave or order your meal. With cell phones there is no excuse for someone not calling either you or the venue to explain their situation. Then you can decide if you can wait for them or make other arrangements for another meeting.

Business Gifts

Sometimes it is difficult to determine when we should give gifts to clients, co-workers or a boss. You don't want to seem to be bribing your clients, buying your way into a particular group at work or looking for a promotion from your boss. But it is thoughtful to thank people for their help or service or for introducing you to a new client and to congratulate clients or co-workers on special occasions or at the completion of a successful project. Whatever the situation, your gift should be a sincere, well thought out and within your budget.

Be aware of how others may react to your gift. If your company is cutting back on expenditures and possibly even downsizing, spend your gift budget cautiously and appropriately.

If you are sharing gifts with people at work, then they should be exchanged in the office or at a special event. Do not send gifts to a home and make sure the gifts are appropriate and do not send the wrong message.

No Gifts Please

For a retirement party or a party to honor an important associate or client, putting "No gifts, please" on an invitation sends a negative connotation. A gentler way of declining gifts is to explain it when the guests RSVP. Still, some guests may want to bring gifts to show their appreciation. If gifts are received, they should not be opened at the party. If you wish to give a gift, you can always send it to the honoree before or after the event.

Another suggestion is to state on the invitation "In lieu of gift, your presence is all we need." Or "In lieu of gifts, donations may be made to the American Cancer Society (or some other charitable organization)."

Giveaway/Amenities

Promotional products are given away at trade shows and are available to sales teams to leave with clients. You can spend from $1 or less to $100 or more on promotional gifts, depending on whether you distribute them to hundreds at a trade show or give them individually to top clients.

Display your company logo on your items but place it discreetly because some people may choose not to wear or use your gift if the logo is too large. Be a little less conspicuous if you want to see people carrying around the bags you gave them or wearing your jacket or golf shirt year after year.

Choosing and Presenting Gifts

- The best gifts are ones that are chosen with the recipient in mind. Know your clients and staff and give appropriate gifts. It makes no sense to give a box of golf balls to a non-golfer or a plant to someone who has a "brown thumb."
- If a woman is sending a male co-worker a gift, she should send the gift to his office with a nice note. But if she was invited to his home, she should send the flowers or gift to his home addressed to both him and his wife.
- Send flowers the following day as a thank-you instead of bringing them the night of a party. Chances are the host has already decorated the home and needs to concentrate on the meal and the guests, rather than to stop and find a vase to display your gift. Flowers arriving the next morning would show appreciation for the host's work.
- Don't bring wine to a party and expect your hosts to open the wine and drink it that night. It is a gift for them to enjoy after the party and not for you to drink at the party.
- If you are sending flowers or perishable gifts, make sure the recipients are home or in the office to accept them. Sending food to the office is always good. It can and should be shared with co-workers. But be careful if sending gifts to the office. They leave room for discussion, speculation and possibly bad office morale.
- Liquor is also a good gift but make sure the recipient drinks and prefers the type of alcohol you select. Someone who does not drink could be offended by a gift of alcohol, and if you send vodka to someone who drinks only gin, it will be obvious that you did not research your gift.

- Gift certificates are great. Although they may seem a little less personal, if you choose a service or product tailored to the tastes or interests of the recipient, gift certificates will be appreciated. A gift card is a smart route.
- Be aware if a client or company can, in fact, receive gifts. Some company and government policies do not allow employees to accept gifts above a specified value.
- Receiving a gift does not mean you have to give one in return. There are times when people just want to show their appreciation. Accept the gift, be happy that they thought to buy you one and send a thank-you note.
- Executive staff may be invited to everything. As an executive, you do not have to attend each celebration or send a gift, but a nice, handwritten note would be appropriate.
- Who should give gifts at Christmas or other holidays? Does the boss give a gift or something to the employees and do the employees give gifts to their boss? Of course, each office is different but generally a boss will give their employees a gift or at least recognition for their dedication to the company. This could be a special dinner, luncheon, an extra day off or individual gifts. Employees do not have to buy or exchange gifts with the boss. But a nice suggestion is for the employees to come together and jointly provide a gift to their immediate boss or CEO. A gift is not how much money you can spend but a gift to show your appreciation. Your gift should be from the heart and could even be homemade cookies or something simple to express your gratitude.
- Most offices do not have rules and regulations about giving gifts among co-workers. Use your good judgment in deciding whether to give gifts or in selecting appropriate gifts for anniversaries, weddings, baby showers and other

occasions.

- Secretary Week is a good time to thank your assistants for their work all year round. Such gifts can be from you individually or from the company.
- Take time to wrap your gift. Don't just throw it in a paper bag you picked up at the convenience store and stuff it with tissue paper you get from the dry cleaner. Make the wrapping as fun as the gift.

Thank-you Notes "3-3-3"

Send thank-you notes promptly to show your appreciation. If you receive a gift from a company or a department, send the note to the president or the head of the department. If 10 people send you one gift, all contributing and signing their names, you should send a thank-you note to each one of them.

The thank-you note is personal, simple, and timely. This note, like all correspondence, reflects one's taste and character. Write neatly (or print) legibly on letter sheets, informals (fold-over notes) or correspondence cards. The thank-you note, an often-overlooked gesture, is critical in creating relationships and personal connections. A thank-you note sent immediately after an event or presentation of a gift could set you apart from your competition.

A simple but good policy to remember is the "3-3-3" format. It takes approximately three minutes to write a thank-you note. The thank-you note does not need to be more than three lines to cover your message efficiently. And the last 3 is for three days. You should try to send your thank-you message within three days. If it is sent in four or five days, that is still absolutely fine and much better than three weeks or three months. So remember "3-3-3" for three minutes, three lines and three days.

When you send a thank-you note, be sure to mention the gift, how much you enjoy it or appreciate it and how you are going to use it. It makes the person who gave the gift feel it is appreciated.

Responding to an RSVP

- It is the height of rudeness not to respond to the host of your intention to accept or decline an invitation.
- Reply within three to seven days to a request for response. Whether or not you plan to attend, it is still very important to respond.
- If you accepted an invitation and discover at the last minute you cannot attend, make every effort to contact the host as soon as possible even if it is the day of the event. Here are other options:
  - Call the location of the event and speak with the general manager, maitre d' or the hotel banquet manager and insist your message be passed to the host. You don't have to talk to the host personally, but make sure the message is given.
  - Write a note to the host the next day explaining your "no-show."
  - Call the host the next day to explain and apologize.
  - If you are called out of town on business, send an apology from that city and call when you return.
- Never bring a guest. If your invitation states only your name then only you are invited. Do not call your host to ask if you can bring along some extra friends. Of course, you cannot. But perhaps the event is an outdoor party

and space is not a factor and it is a "come and go" type event. Then and only then could you call and explain that you have an unexpected guest in town and ask if they would mind if you brought that person along. If the party or event is in a ticketed area, then you should offer to pay for your guest. If it is a smaller, intimate dinner party, then just express your apologies because you cannot attend because of the house guest and hopefully you could arrange for a luncheon or another get-together at a later time.

- Be on time. Don't arrive at 7:40 p.m. for an event that was scheduled from 6:30 p.m. to 8:00 p.m. Being fashionably late is long gone.   It is very rude if the party is in someone's home. They have their evening planned and it's difficult to wait on just one or two people.
- Be considerate of the host/hostess. They worked and planned to coordinate this function and you don't need to add to their burden by not responding and bringing uninvited guests.

Extending Invitations with RSVPs

- R.S.V.P., RSVP or R.s.v.p. are all correct.
- A deadline for RSVP may be given. But don't wait to respond minutes before the deadline. The host and/or hostess need as much time as possible to plan the event or party. It is also extremely costly and time consuming to have to call invited guests to see if they will be attending.
- To facilitate responses, be sure to give guests a phone, fax and/or e-mail contact with names and numbers or include a self-addressed card and postage.
- "Acceptance only" and "regrets only" rarely work and send out a negative feeling about the party or event. You

are telling the people that you are inviting that it is fine to decline with "regrets only."

- You can almost calculate that two-thirds of your list will actually show. If it is a rainy, stormy day, subtract as much as half from the list and you will probably have a fairly accurate count.

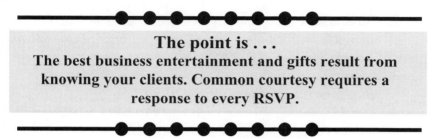

The point is . . .
The best business entertainment and gifts result from knowing your clients. Common courtesy requires a response to every RSVP.

Reading List

1. Letitia Baldridge. *Letitia Baldridge's New Complete Guide to Executive Manners*. Scribner. 1993.
2. Susan Bixler and Nancy Nix-Rice. *The New Professional Image from Business Casual to the Ultimate Power Look*. Adams Media Corp. 1997.
3. Laurie D. Borman. *The Smart Woman's Guide to Business Travel*. Career Press. 1999.
4. Laurel Cardone. *Fodor's How-to-Pack Experts Share Their Secrets*. Fodor's Travel Publications. 1997.
5. Stacie Krajchir and Carrie Rosten. *The Itty Bitty Guide to Tipping*. Chronicle Books. 2004.
6. Mary Mitchell with John Corr. *The Complete Idiot's Guide to Business Etiquette*. Alpha Books. 1999.
7. Barbara Pachter and Marjorie Brody with Betsy Anderson. *Prentice Hall Complete Business Etiquette Handbook*. Prentice Hall Press. 1994.
8. Linda and Wayne Phillips. *The Concise Guide to Executive Etiquette*. Doubleday. 1990.
9. Karyn Repinski. *The Complete Idiot's Guide to Successful Dressing*. Alpha Books. 1999.
10. Ann Marie Sabath. *Business Etiquette: 101 Ways to Conduct Business with Charm and Savvy*. Career Press. 1997.
11. Nat Segaloff. *The Everything Etiquette Book*. Adams Media Corp. 1997.

Colleen Rickenbacher, CMP, CSEP, CPC

—————— ● ● ● ● ● ● ● ——————

A native of Pennsylvania, Colleen Rickenbacher served the Dallas Convention & Visitors Bureau for 15 years as vice president of event planning. She continued for five additional years with the Dallas CVB as a contract event planner and during this time, in 2001, started her own company, Colleen Rickenbacher Inc. (CRI). She continued her work as an independent event planner and speaker.   But after a total of 35 years in the hospitality industry, she is now solely concentrating on presentations, training programs and books.

Over the past 11 years, Rickenbacher has had numerous speaking engagements, including a seminar for the Certified Meeting Professional teaching program in Florence, Italy, a guest lecture at Cornell University School of Hotel Administration in New York and a presentation about customer service to 150 government and city officials in Zimbabwe, Africa.

Rickenbacher is a regular on television and radio programs, including Country Music Television, Fox News, "The Joni Show," "Make Your Day Count" and many local and national T.V. shows and radio programs.

Rickenbacher's speaking topics include all levels and all facets of Business and Dining Etiquette, International Protocol, Appearance and Attitude and Why It Makes a Difference, Leadership, Customer Service, Presentation Skills, Working Out of Your Home, Office Etiquette, How to Add the "Wow!" to Your Next Event, Public Etiquette, Safety at Home and on the Road, Packing Tips for Travel and Connecting and Getting the Best End Results.

To strengthen her skills of etiquette and protocol, Rickenbacher is an Advisory Board member of the International Association of Protocol Consultants (IAPC) headquartered in Washington, D.C. She is one of five people in the world achieving the Certified Protocol Consultant (CPC) designation. Rickenbacher has chaired the Certified Meeting Professional (CMP) Board and served as a member of the Convention Industry Council Board and the Board of Directors of Meeting Professionals International (MPI). She is also a past president of the MPI Dallas/Fort Worth Chapter and was the first president of the Texas Association of Event and Convention Professionals (TxACOM). She also served on the Advisory Board of the International Special Events Society.

Rickenbacher earned a BS in business administration with a minor in international business from Northwood University, where she graduated Magna Cum Laude. She holds the designations of Certified Protocol Consultant (CPC), Certified Meeting

Professional (CMP) and Certified Special Events Professional (CSEP). Rickenbacher was recognized as the "Meeting Partner of the Year" by the National Speakers Association and received the Marion N. Kershner Award from MPI for motivational leadership. She was also named one of "The 25 Most Influential People in the Meetings Industry" by *Meeting News Magazine*. The Colleen Rickenbacher Leadership Award created in her honor annually recognizes an outstanding leader from the MPI Dallas/Fort Worth Chapter and TxACOM created the Colleen Rickenbacher scholarship fund for educational programs. She has won numerous other awards and recognition for her endless service and dedication to teaching and training.

Rickenbacher and her husband, Steve, reside in Dallas. They have three children and three grandchildren.

Visit the author's Web site at www.colleenrickenbacher.com.